Menagerie Macabre

Fever Dreams

An Adult Coloring Book

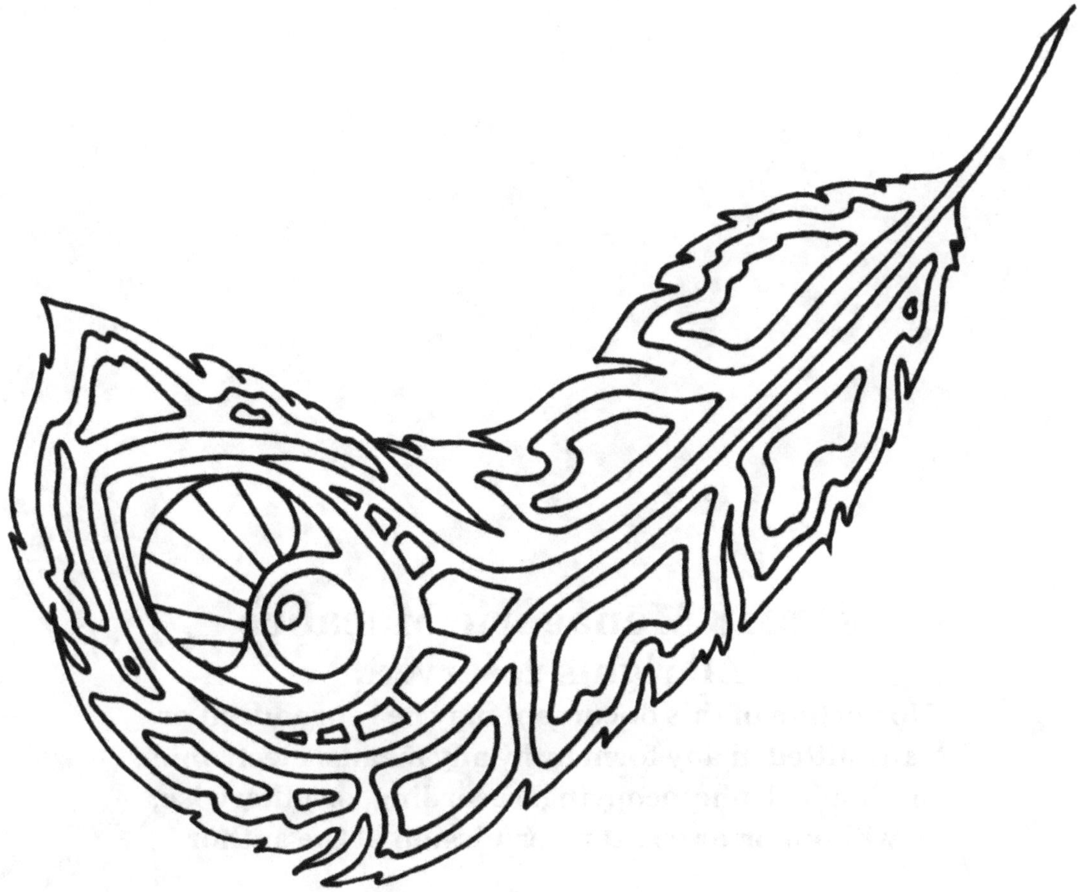

For everyone who believed in me

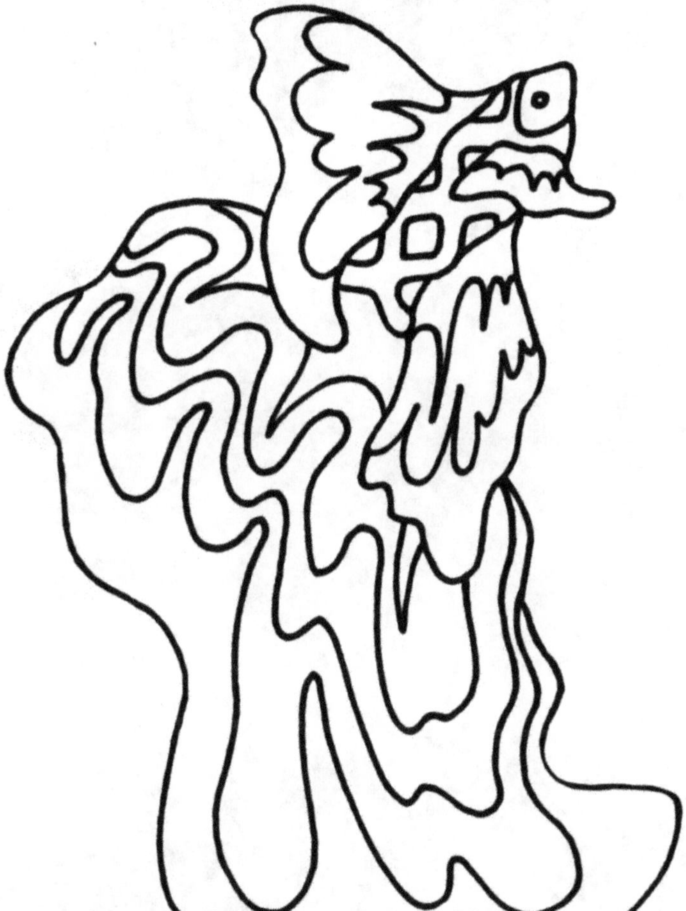

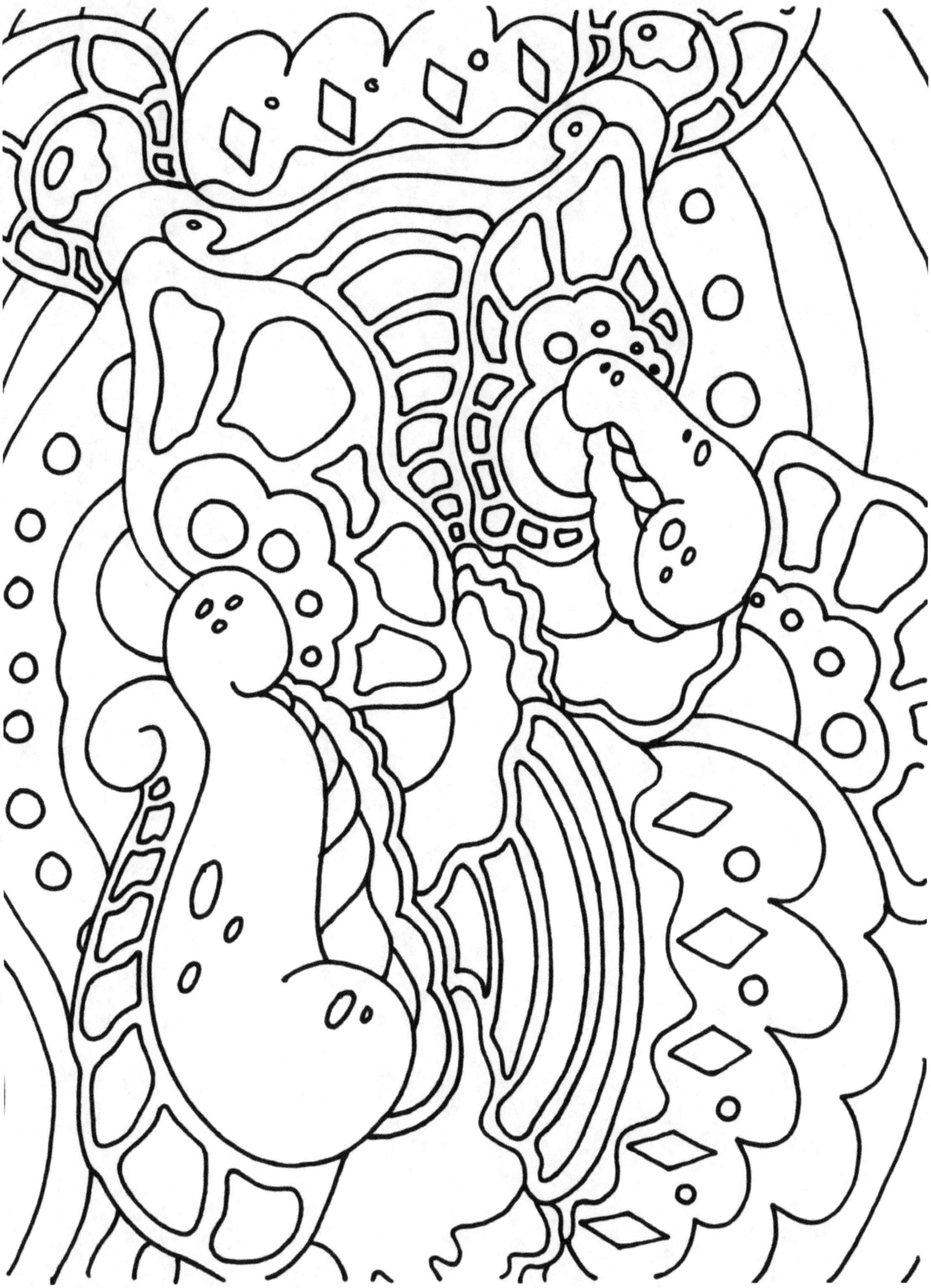

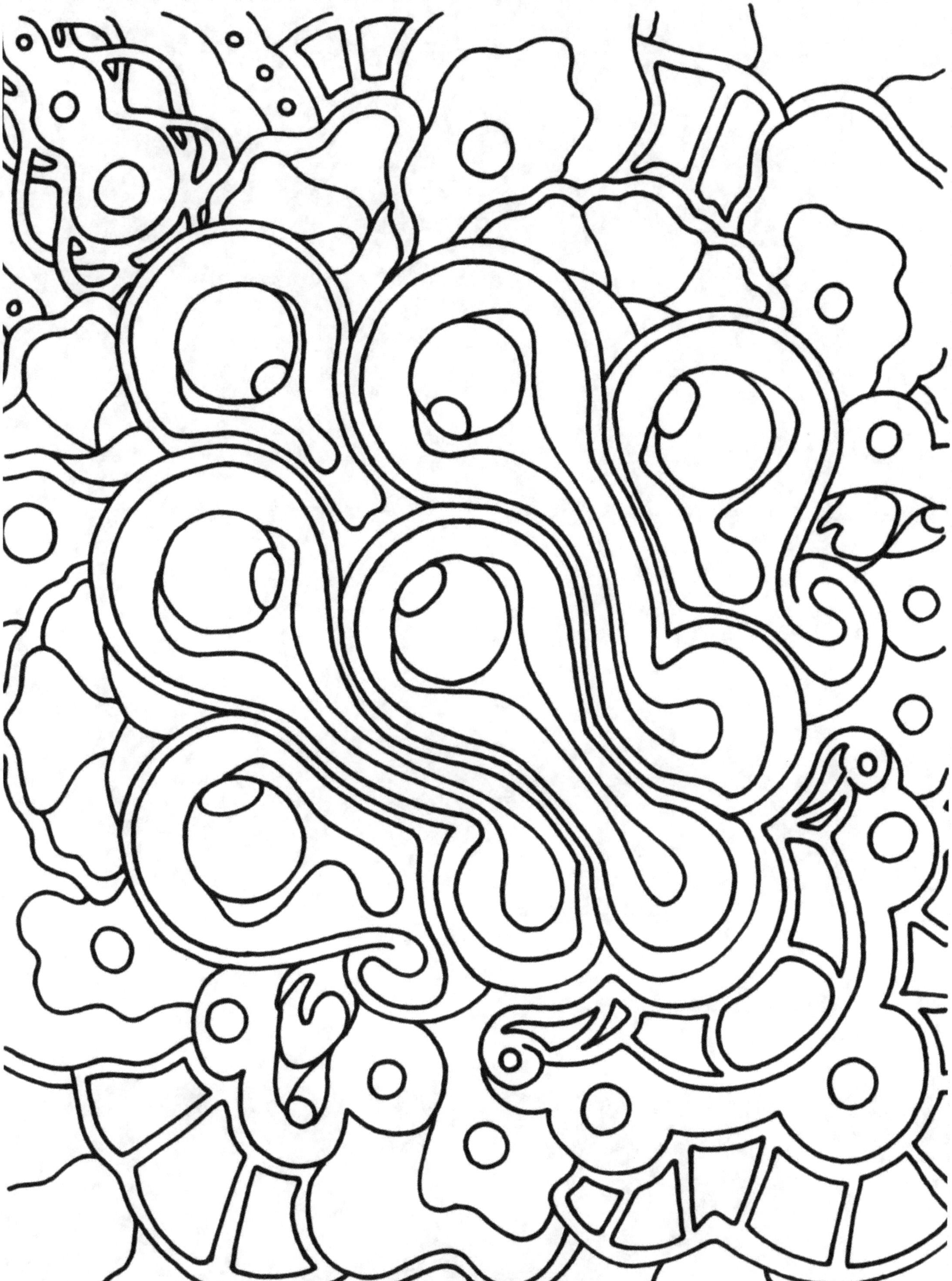

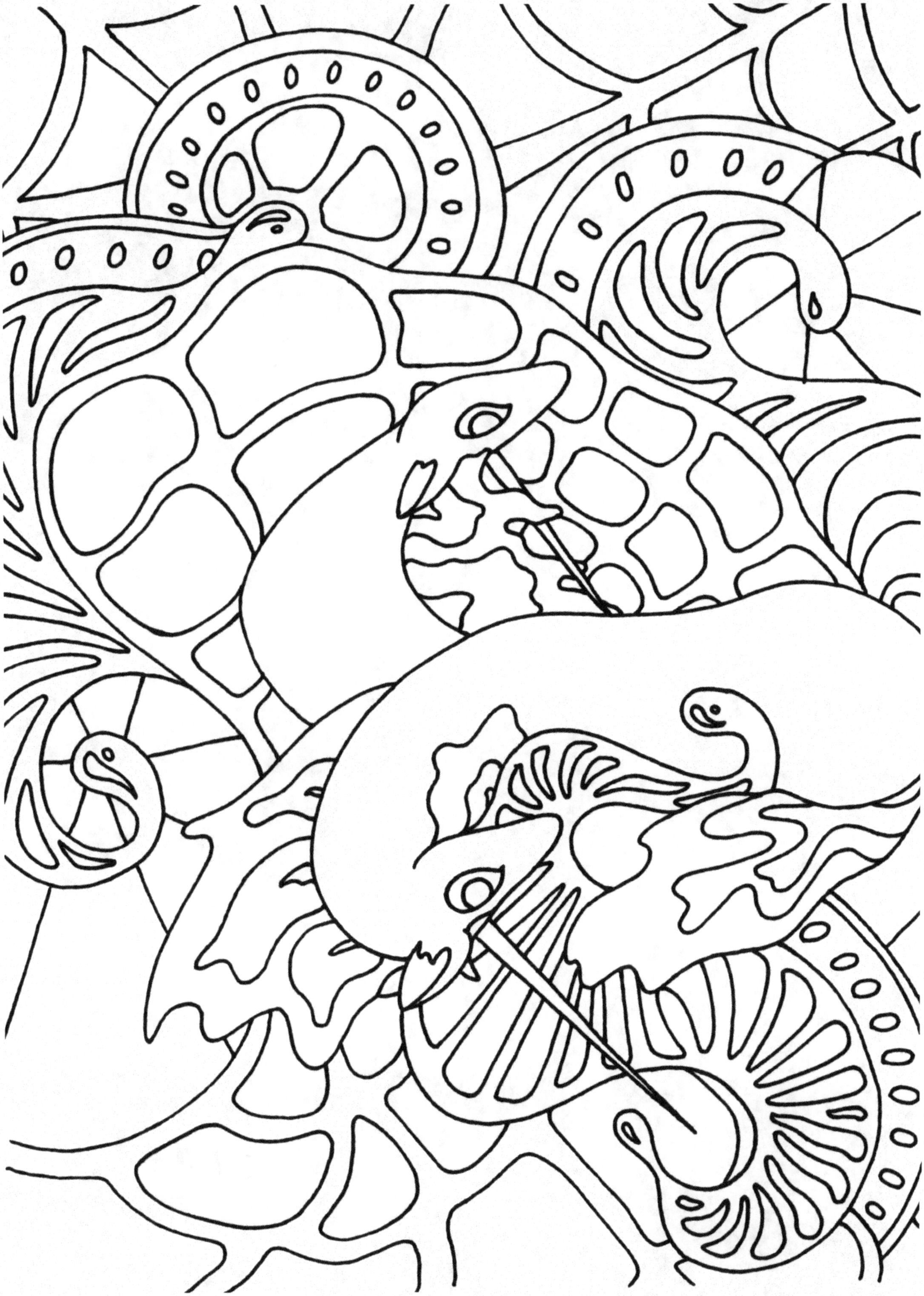

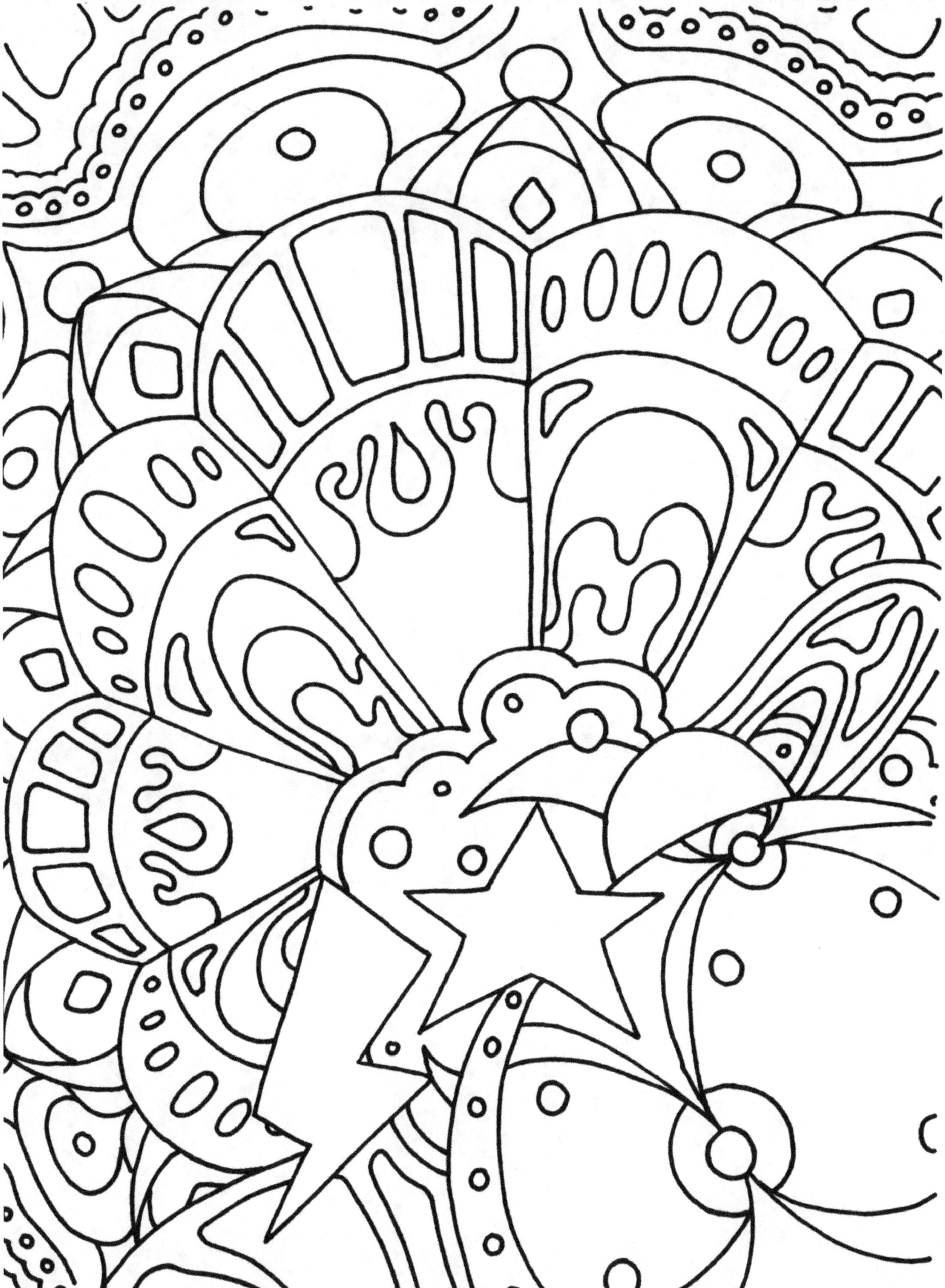

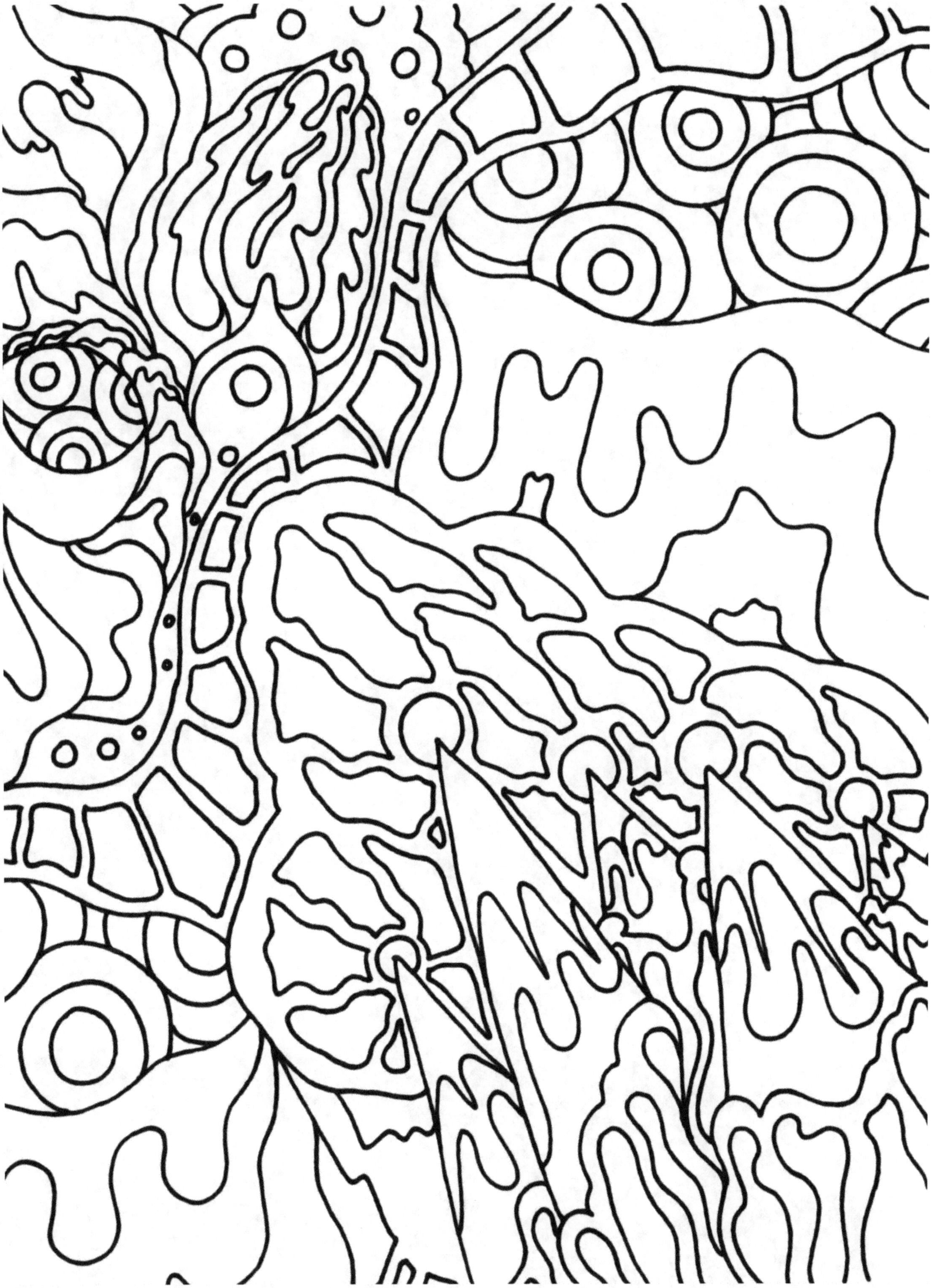

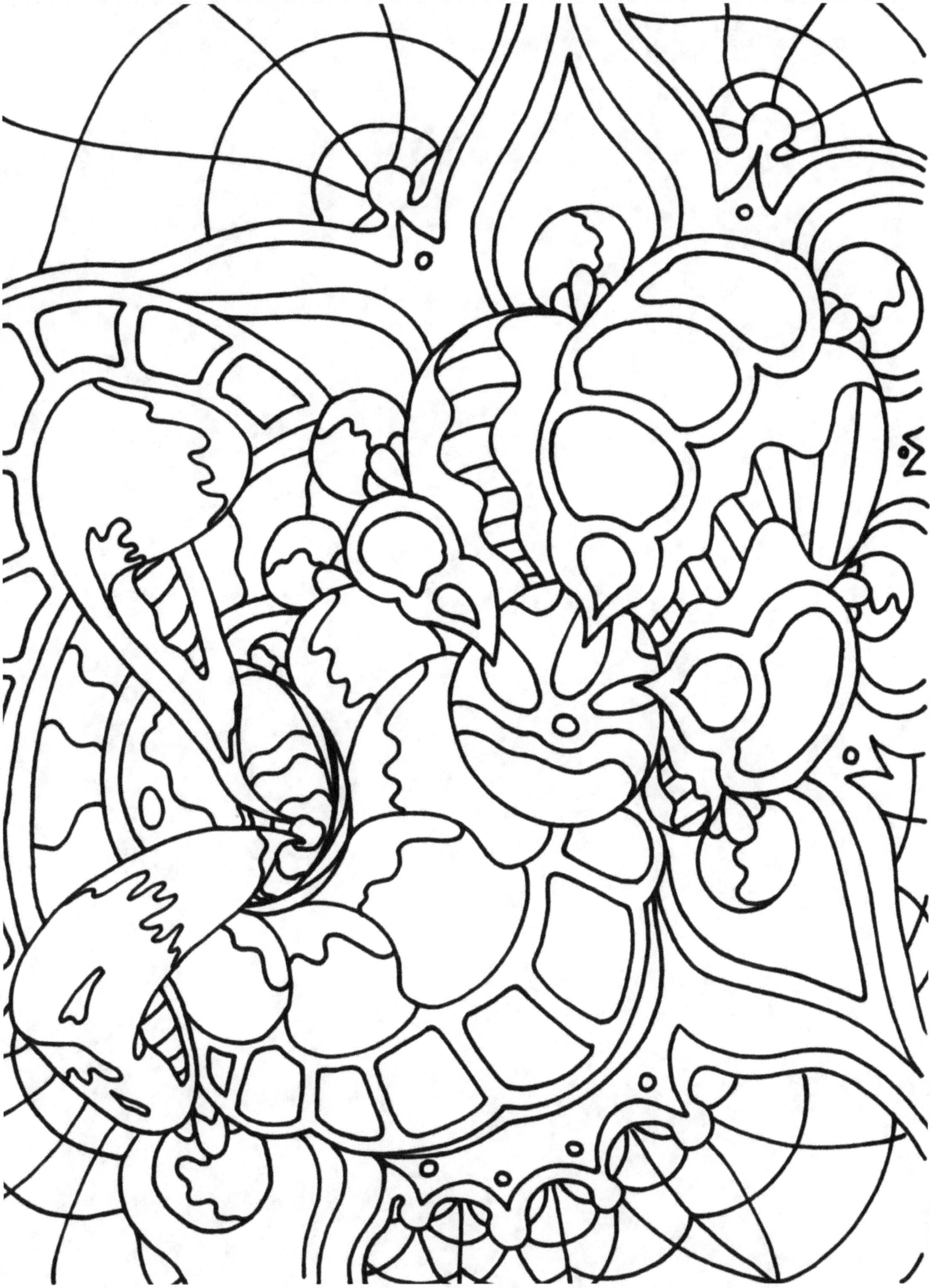

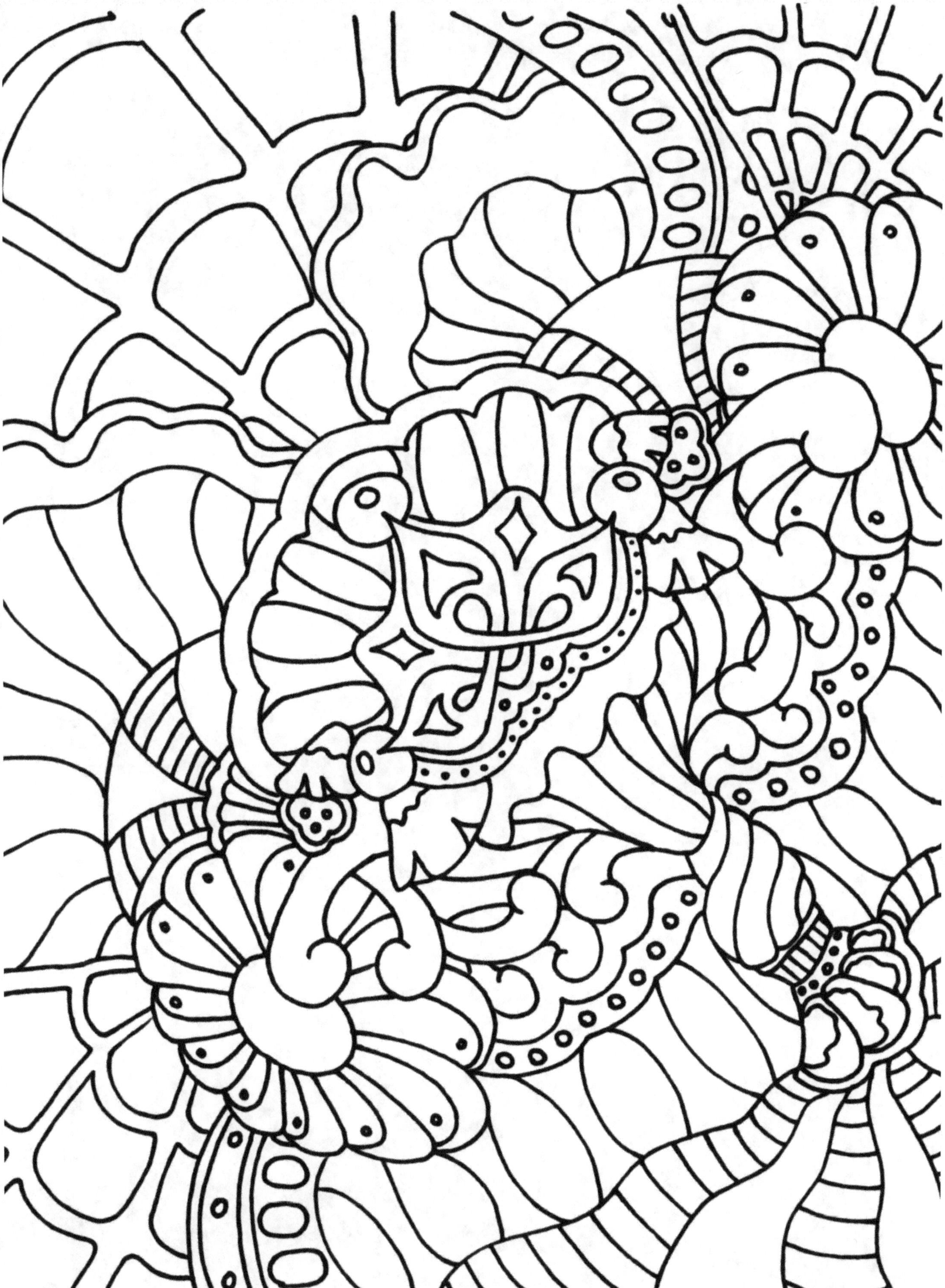

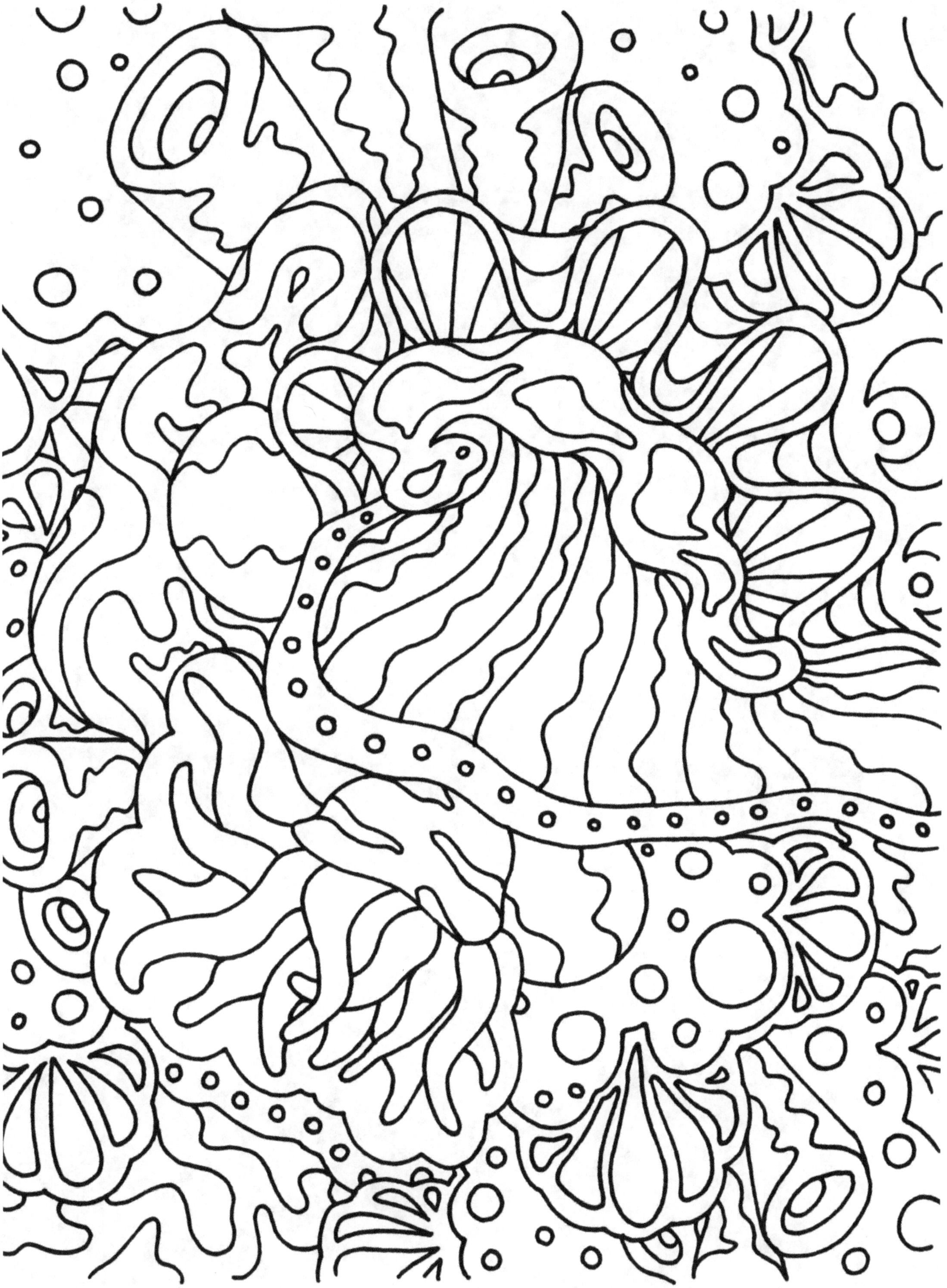

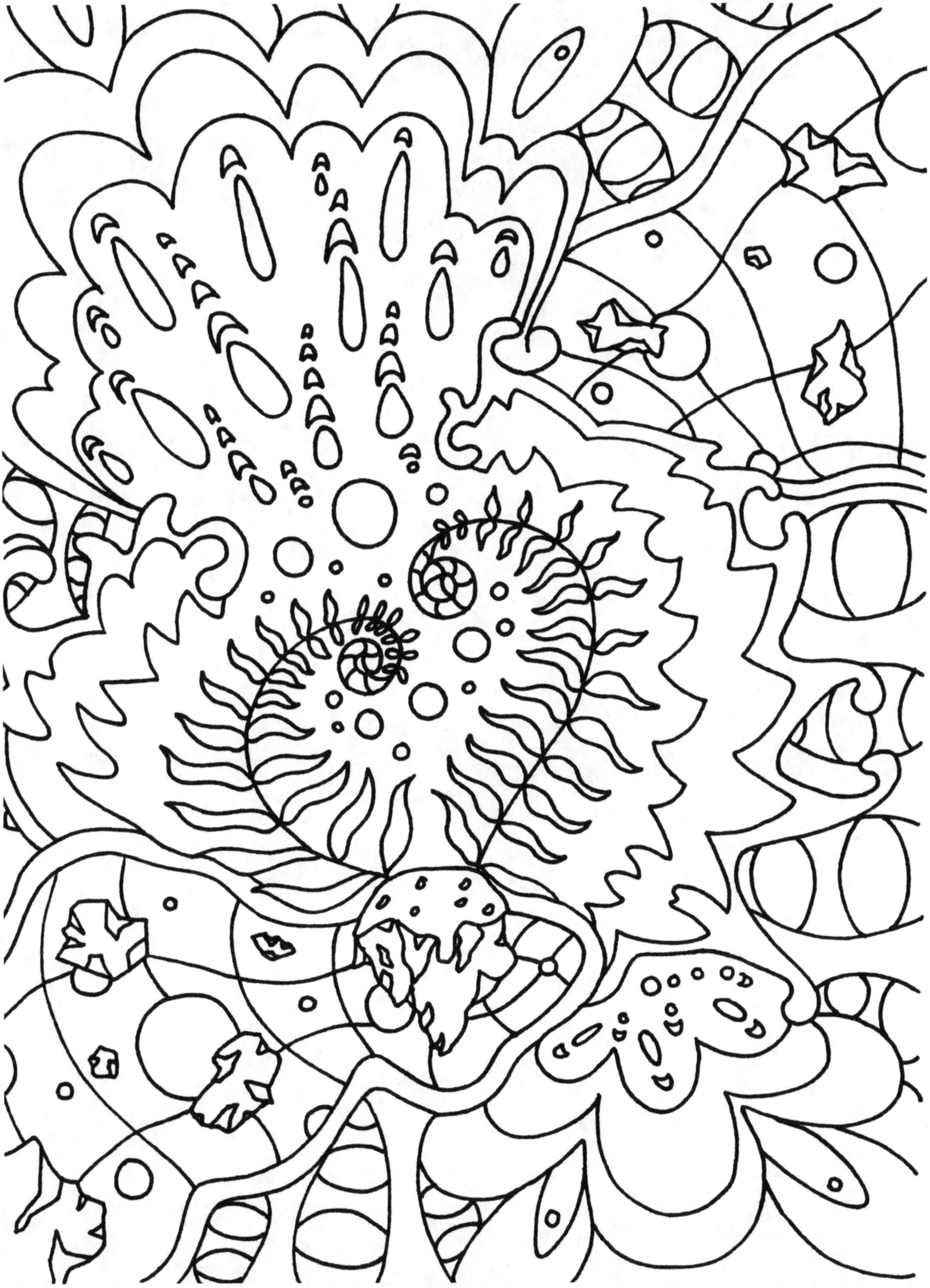

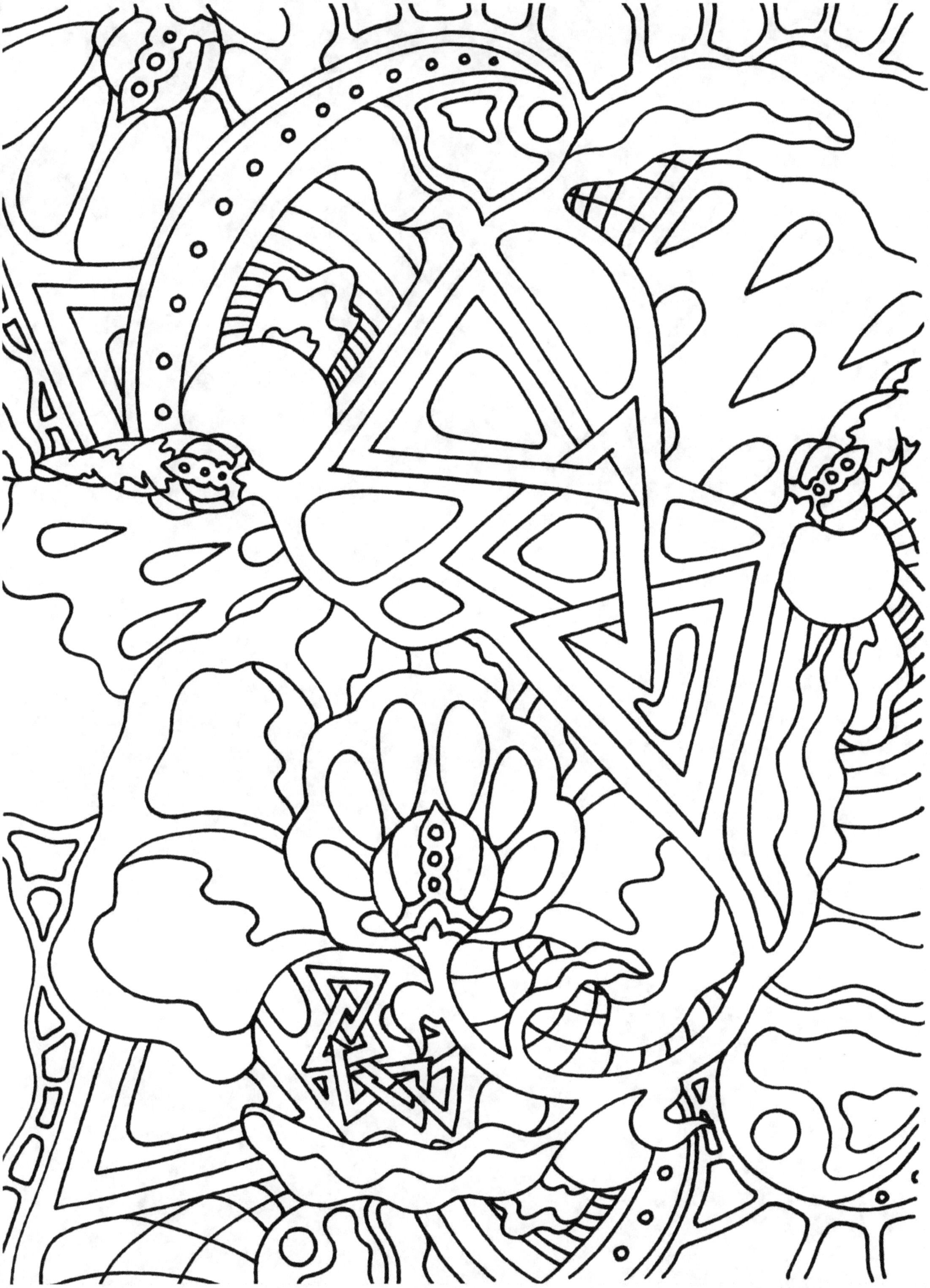

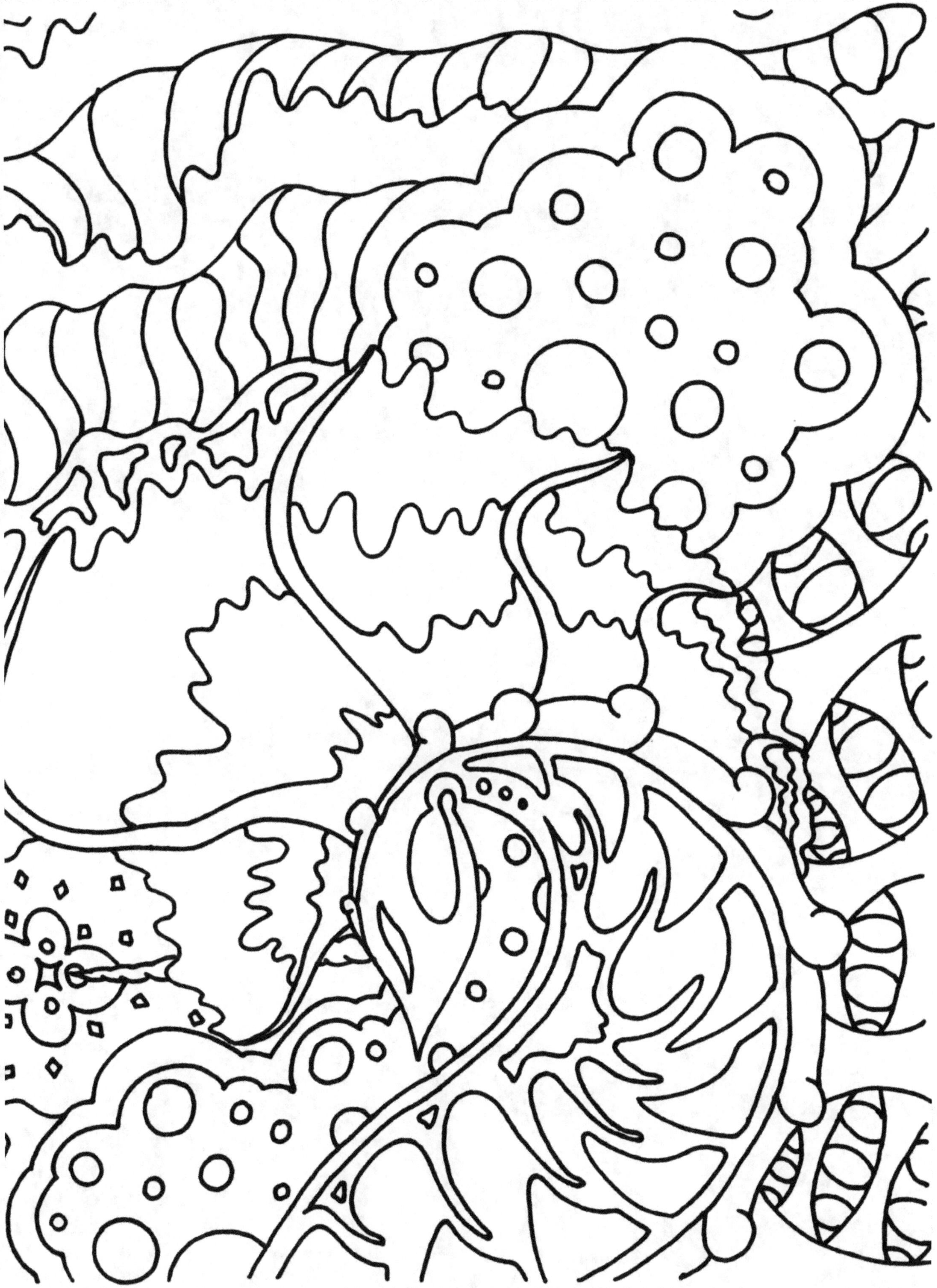

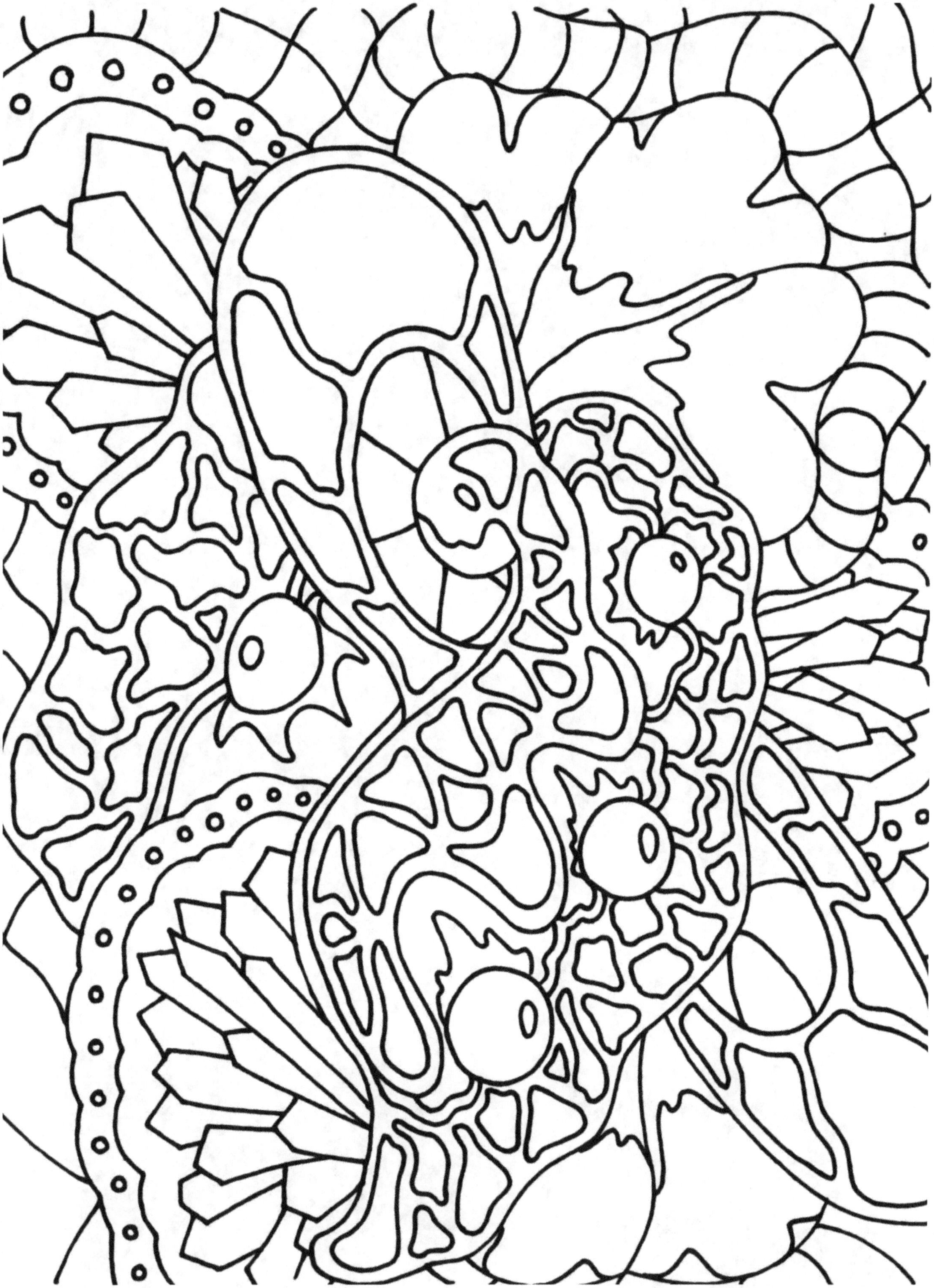

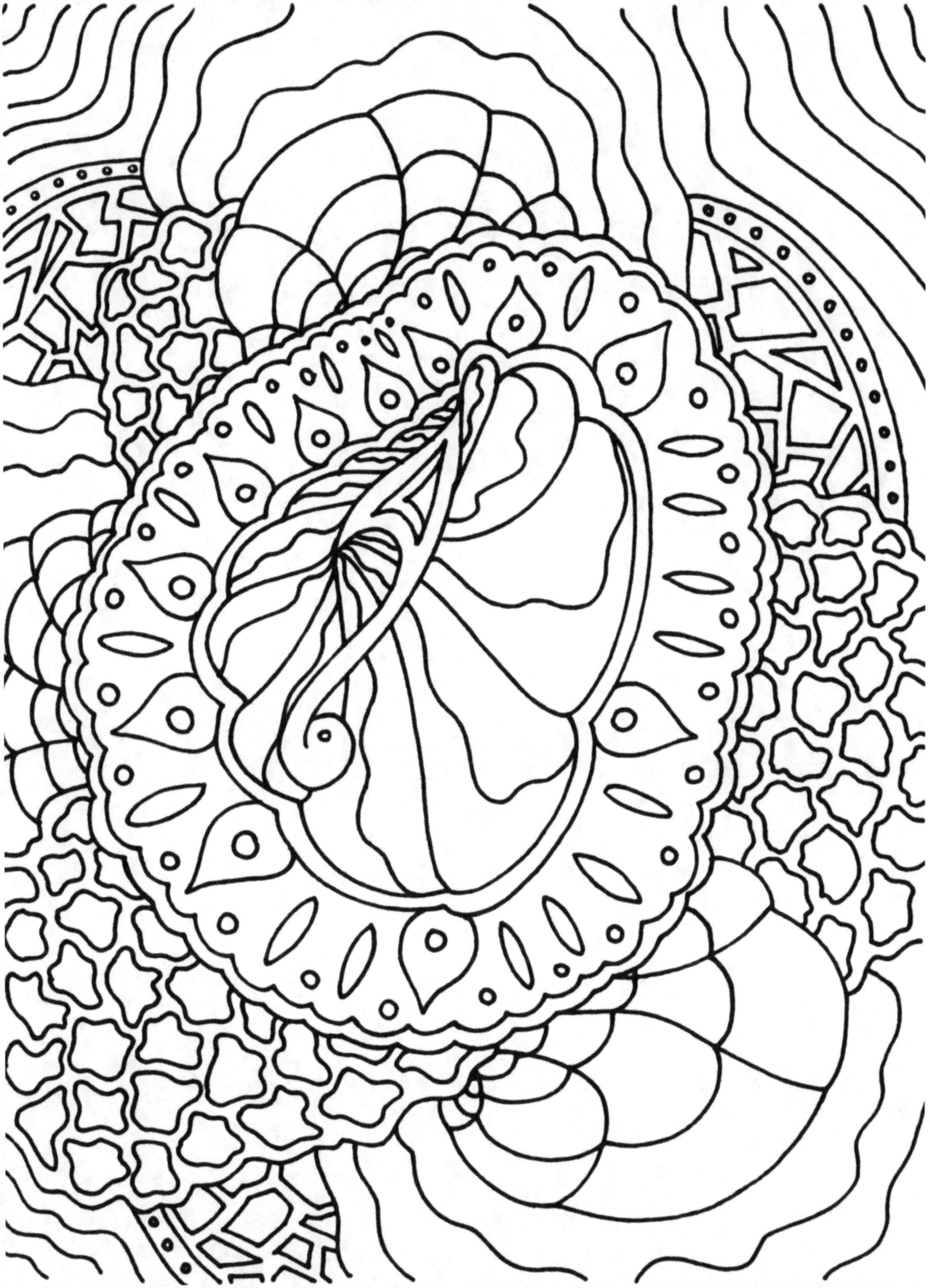

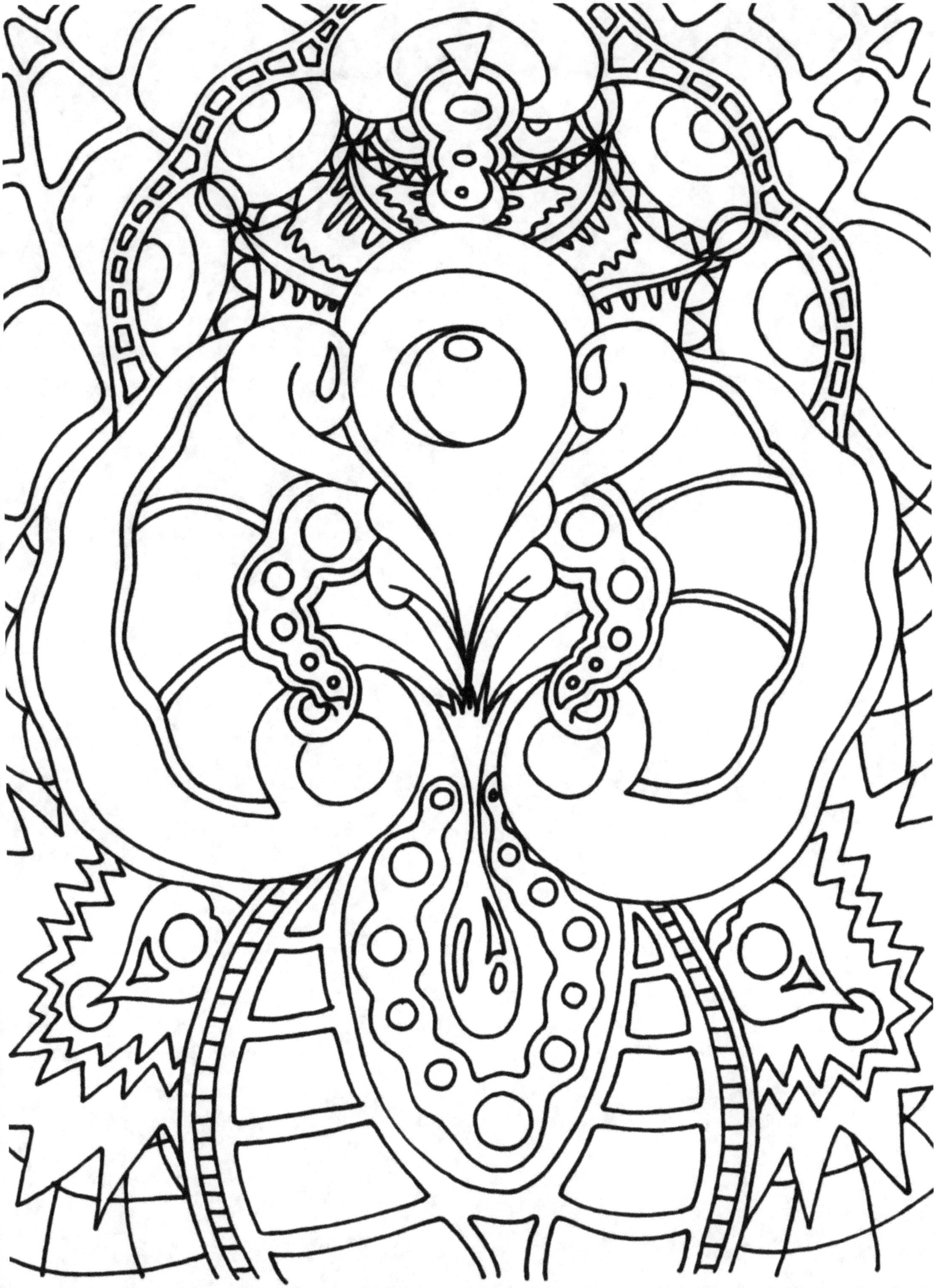

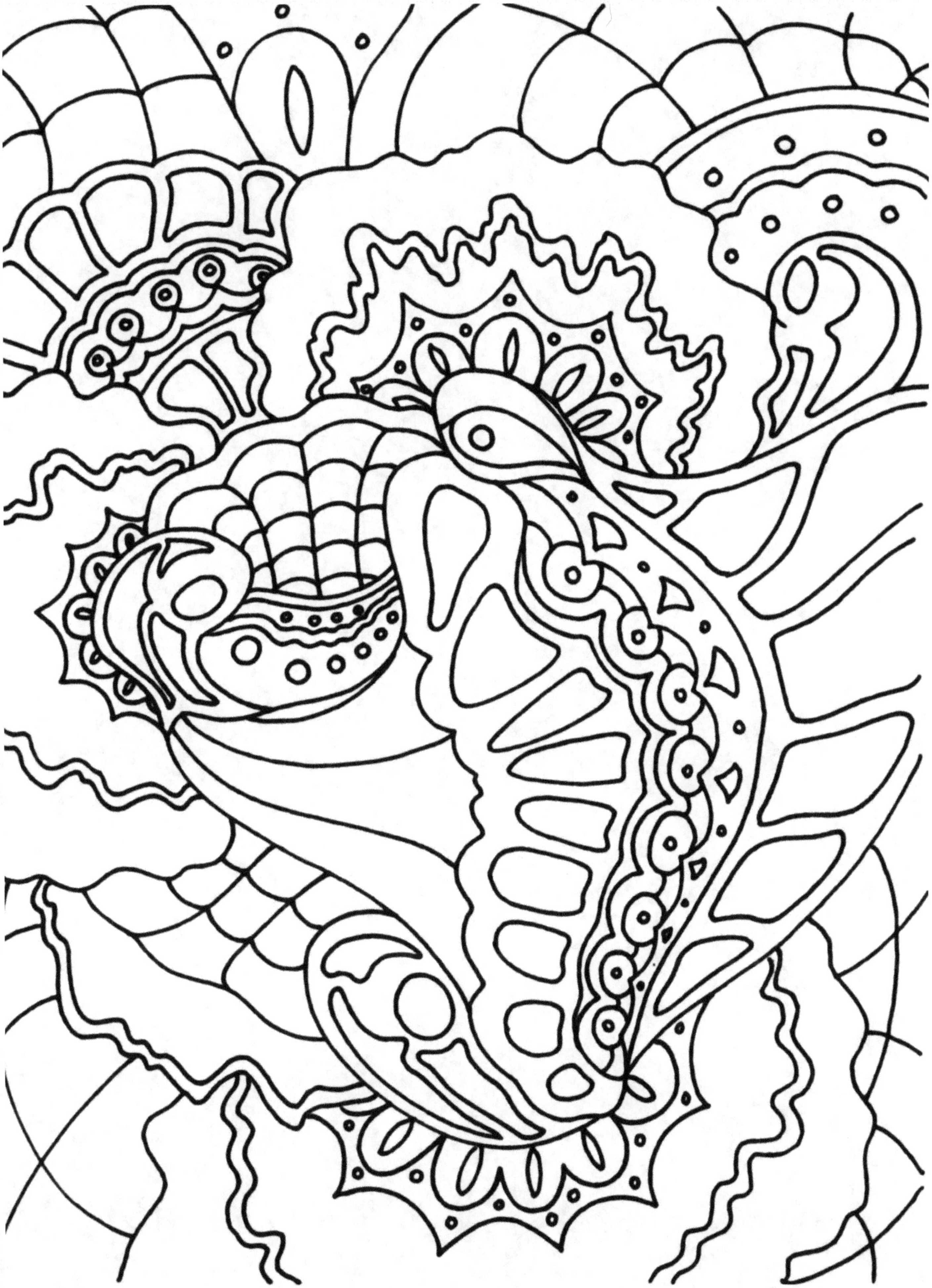

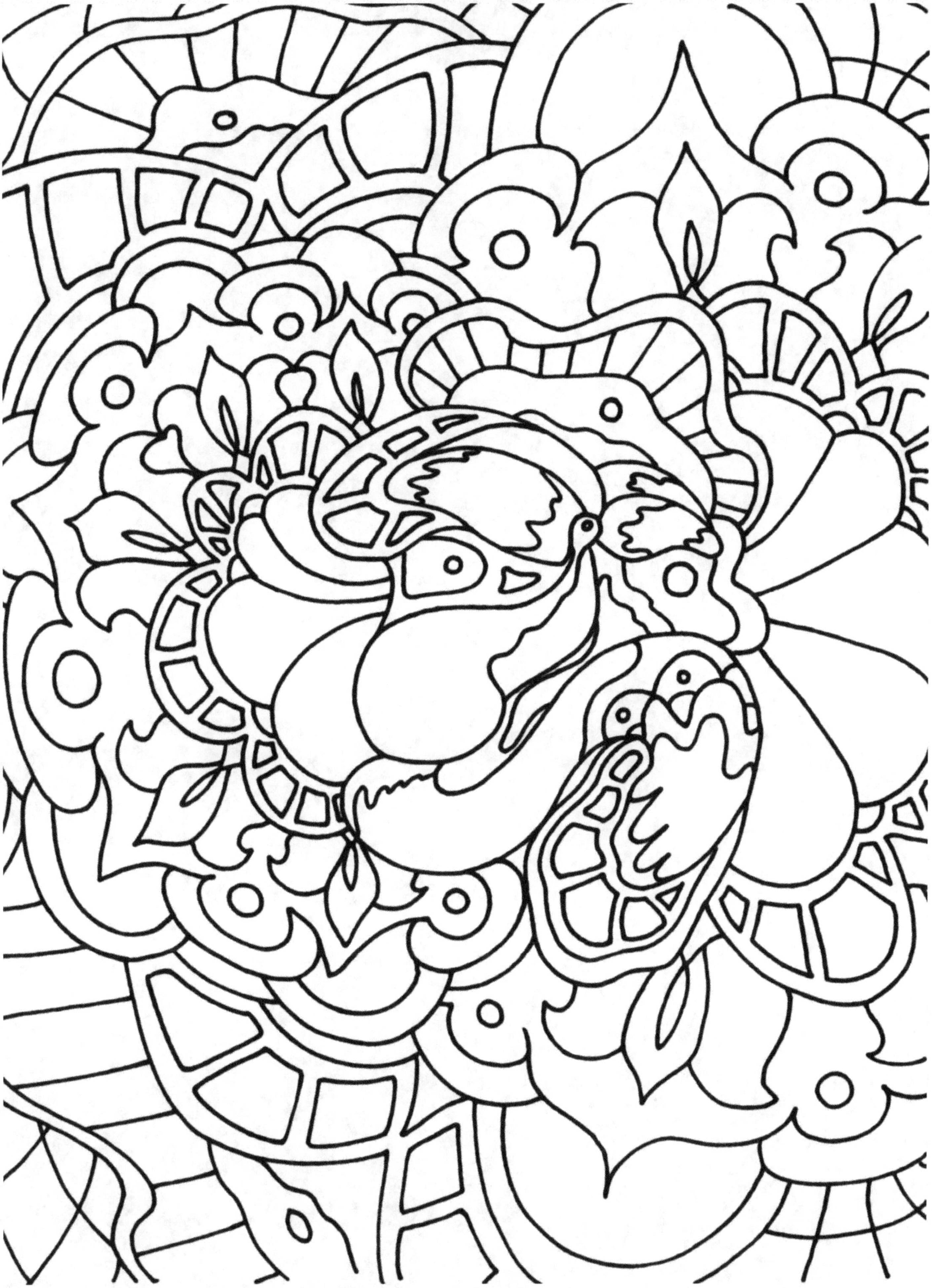

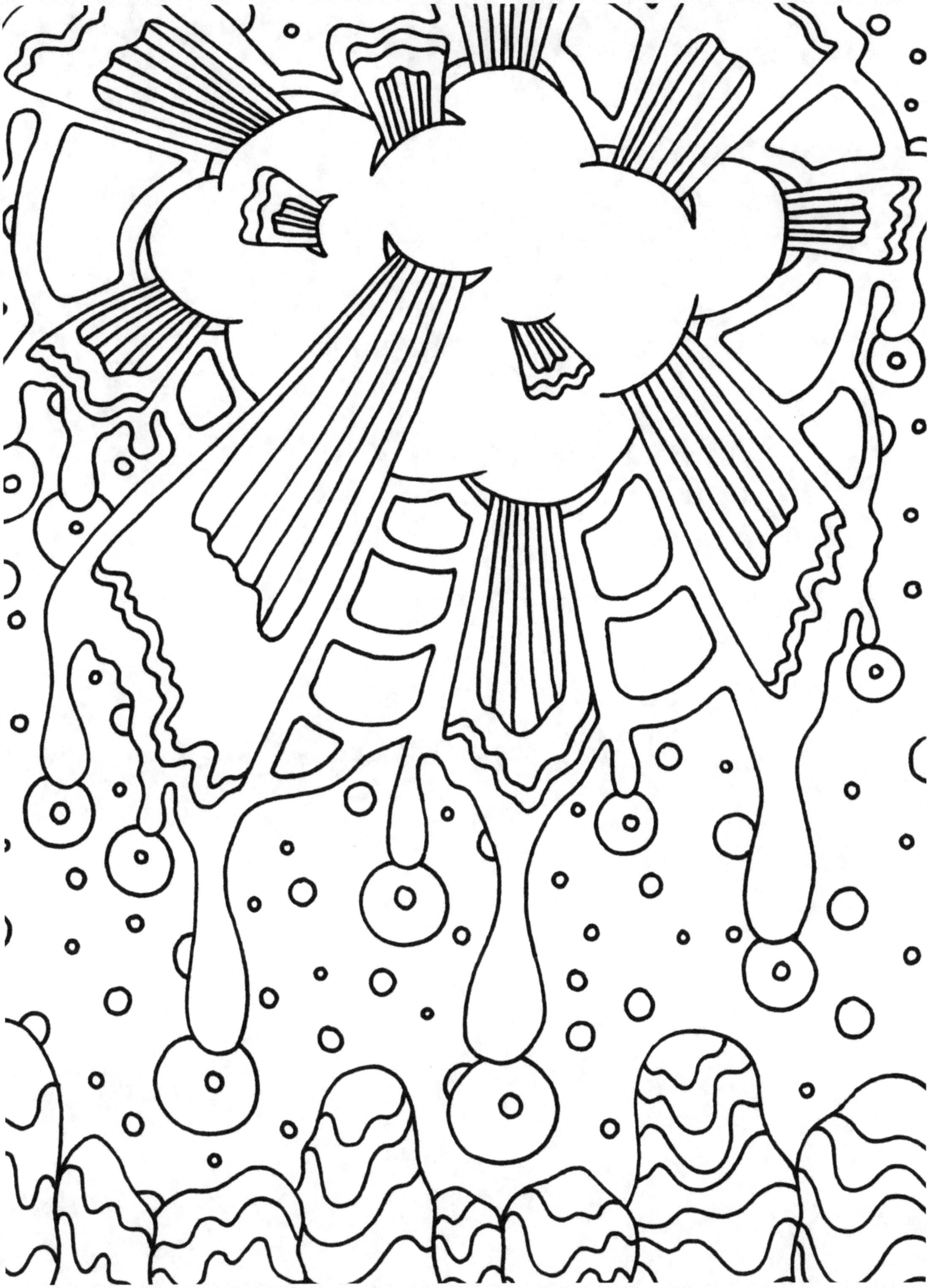

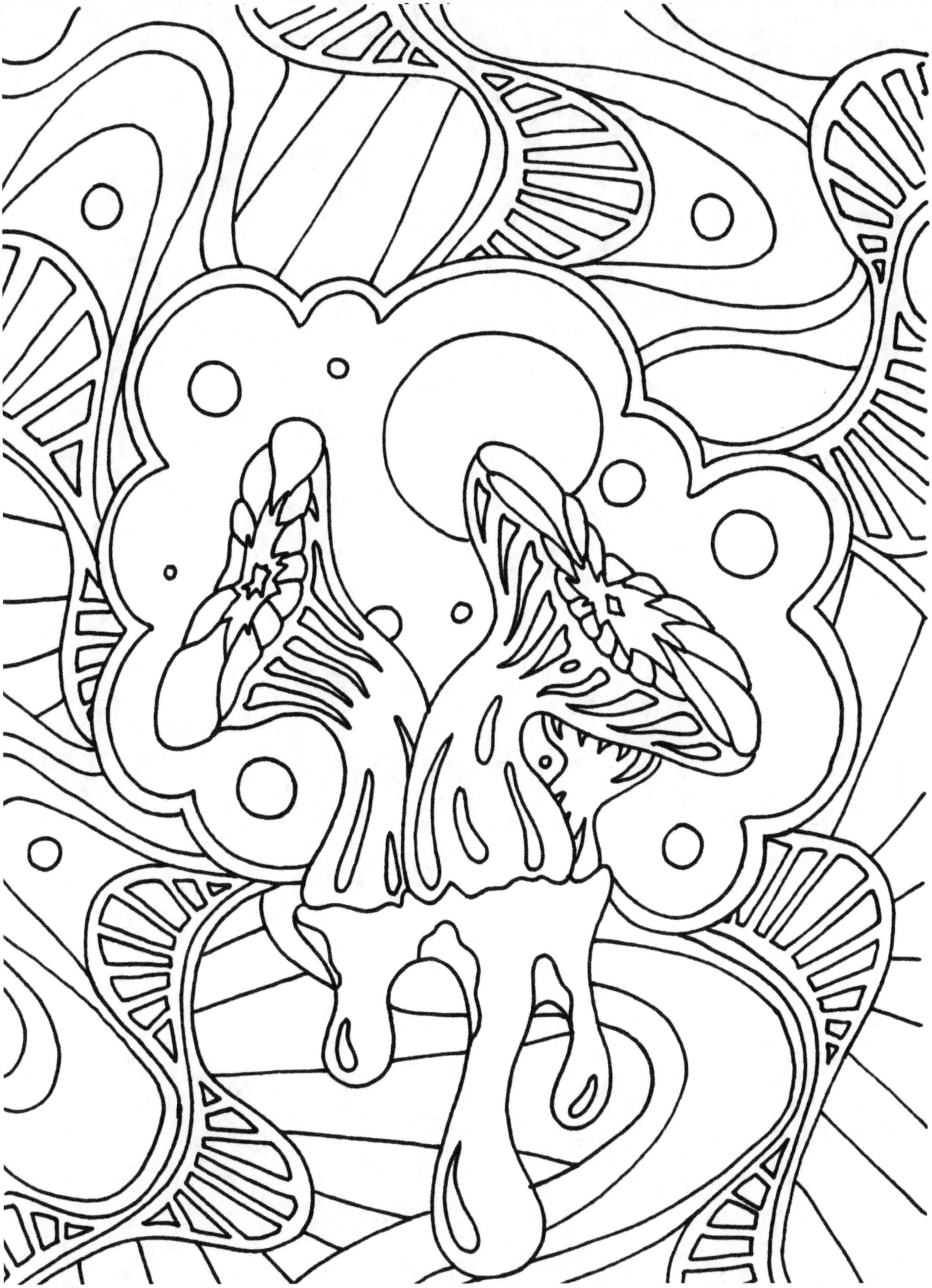

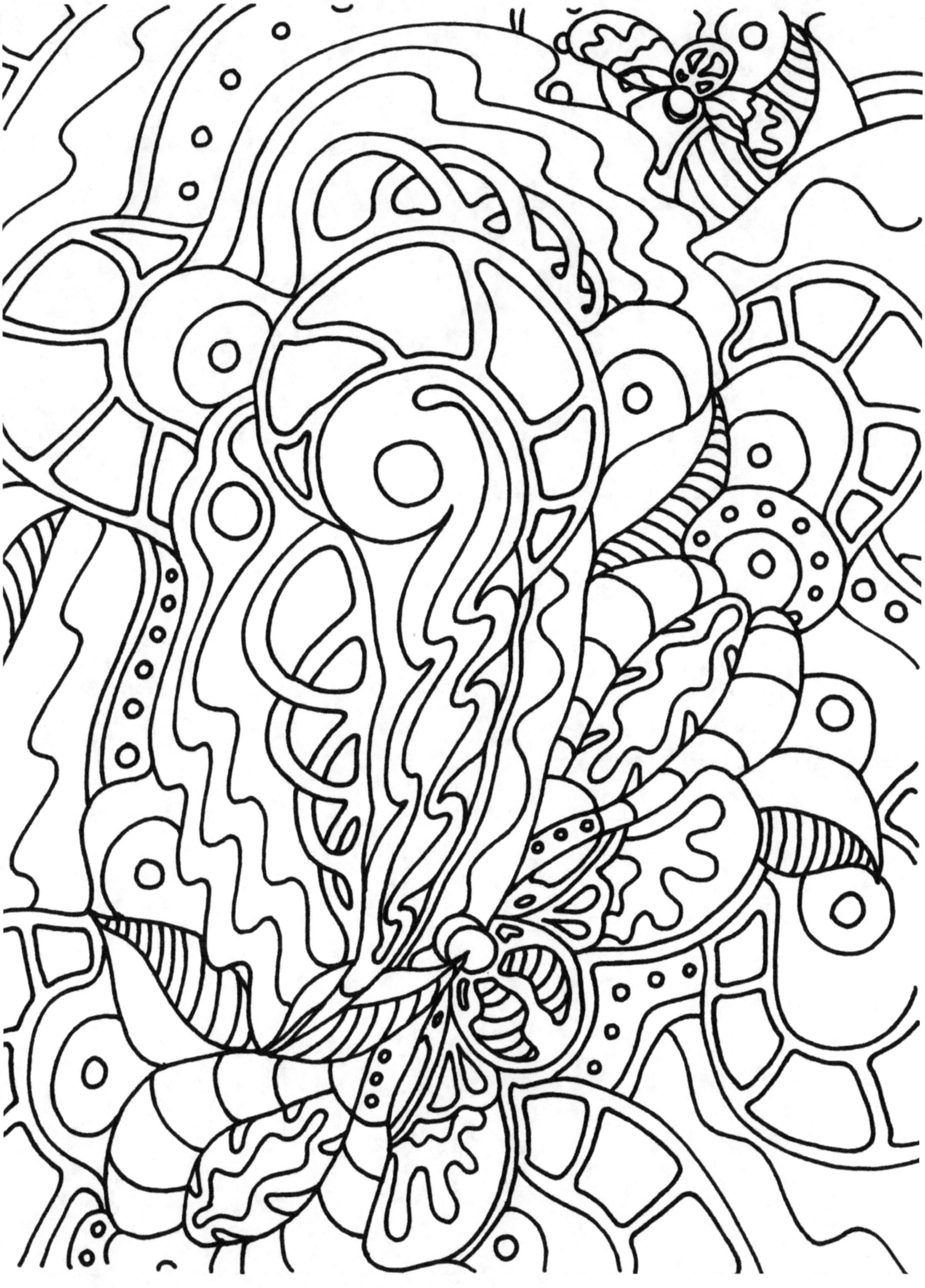

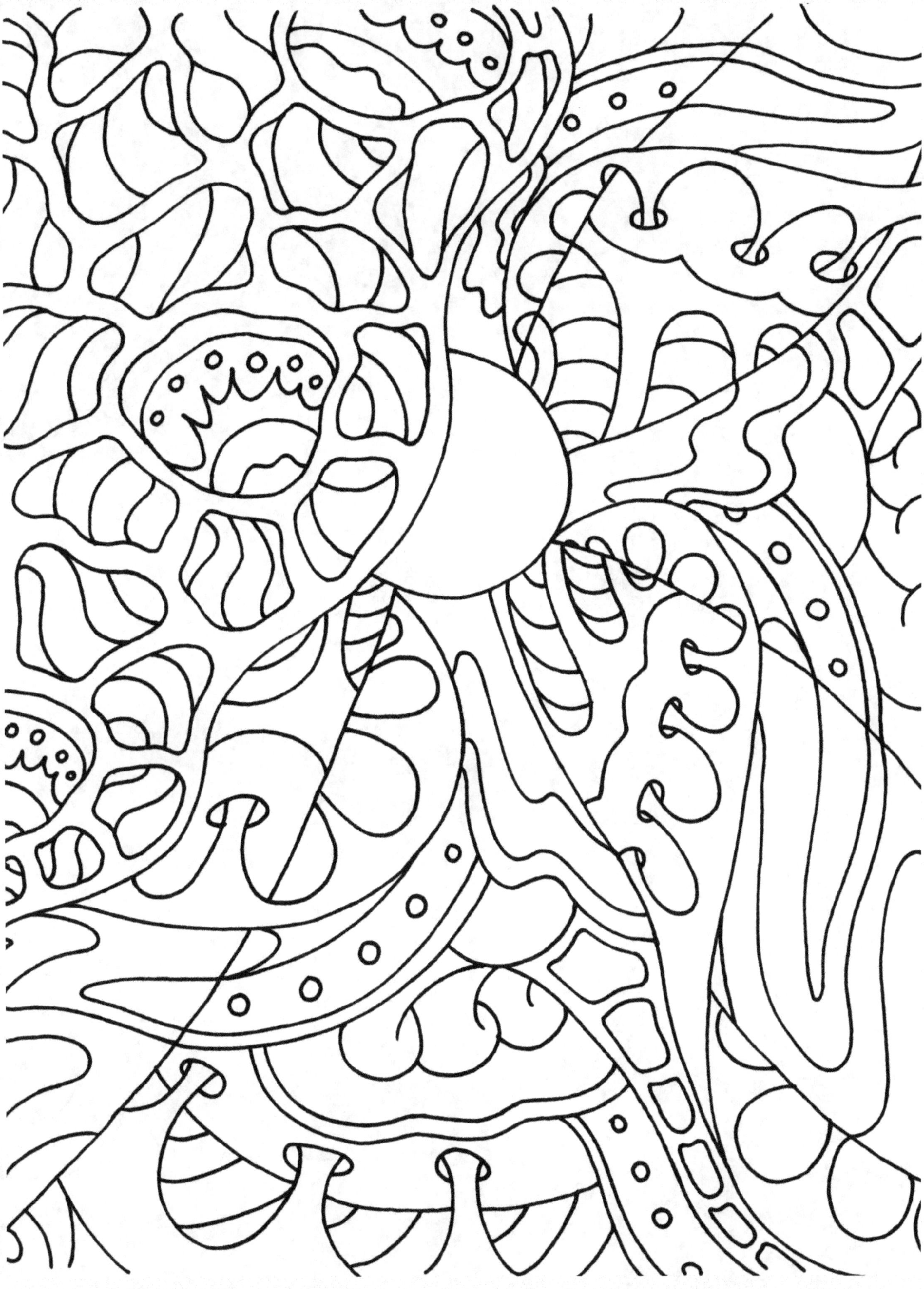

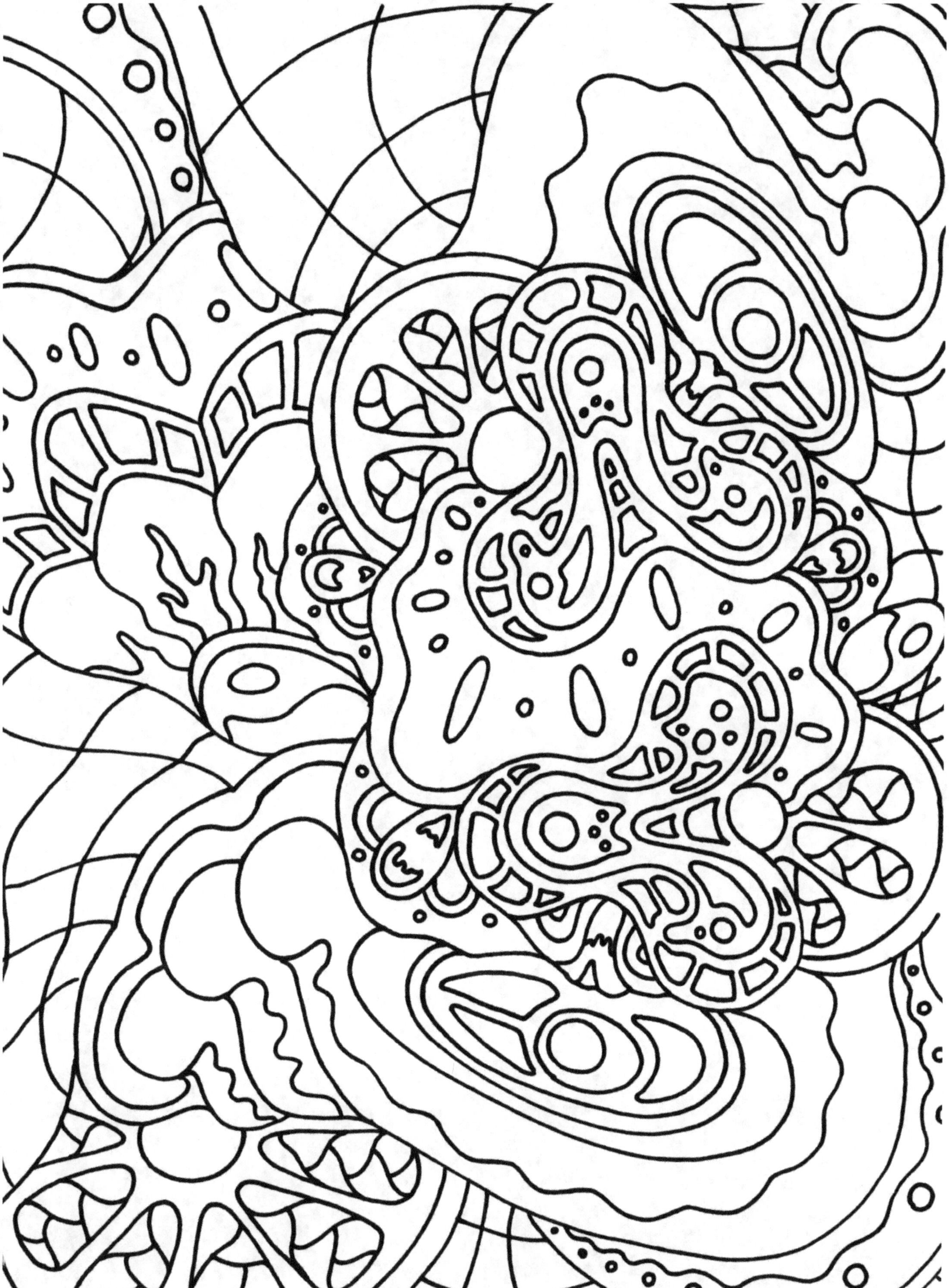

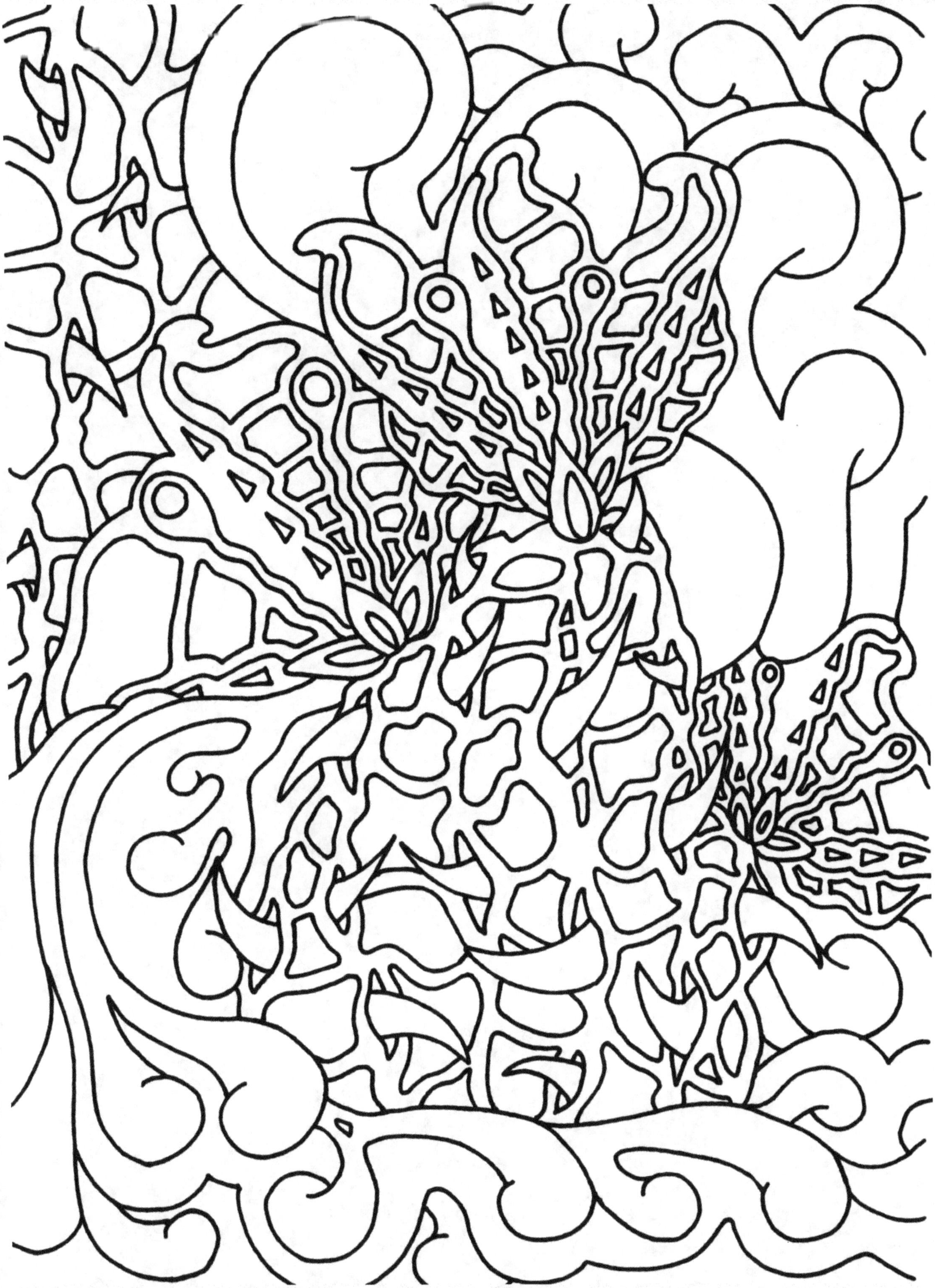

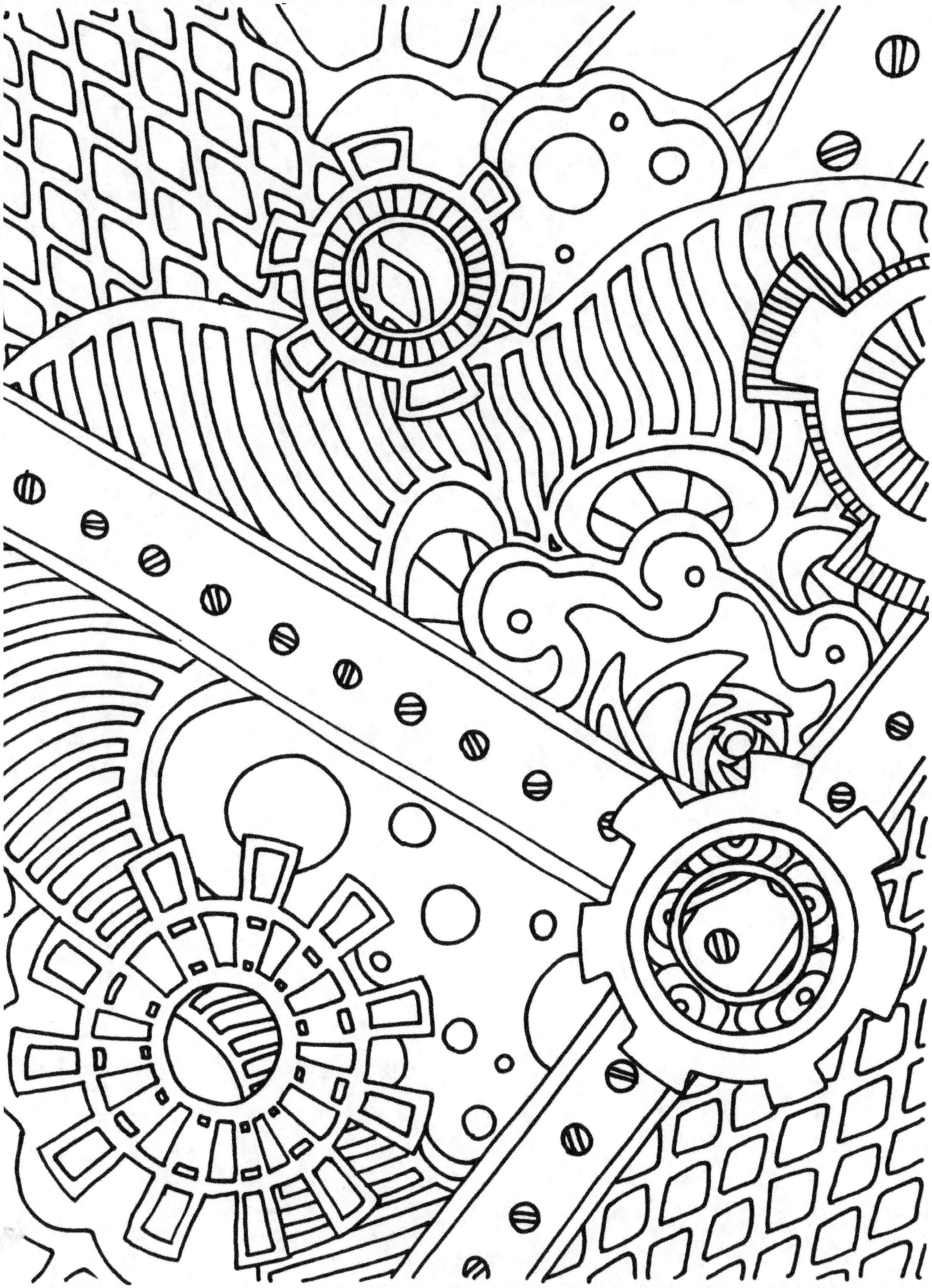

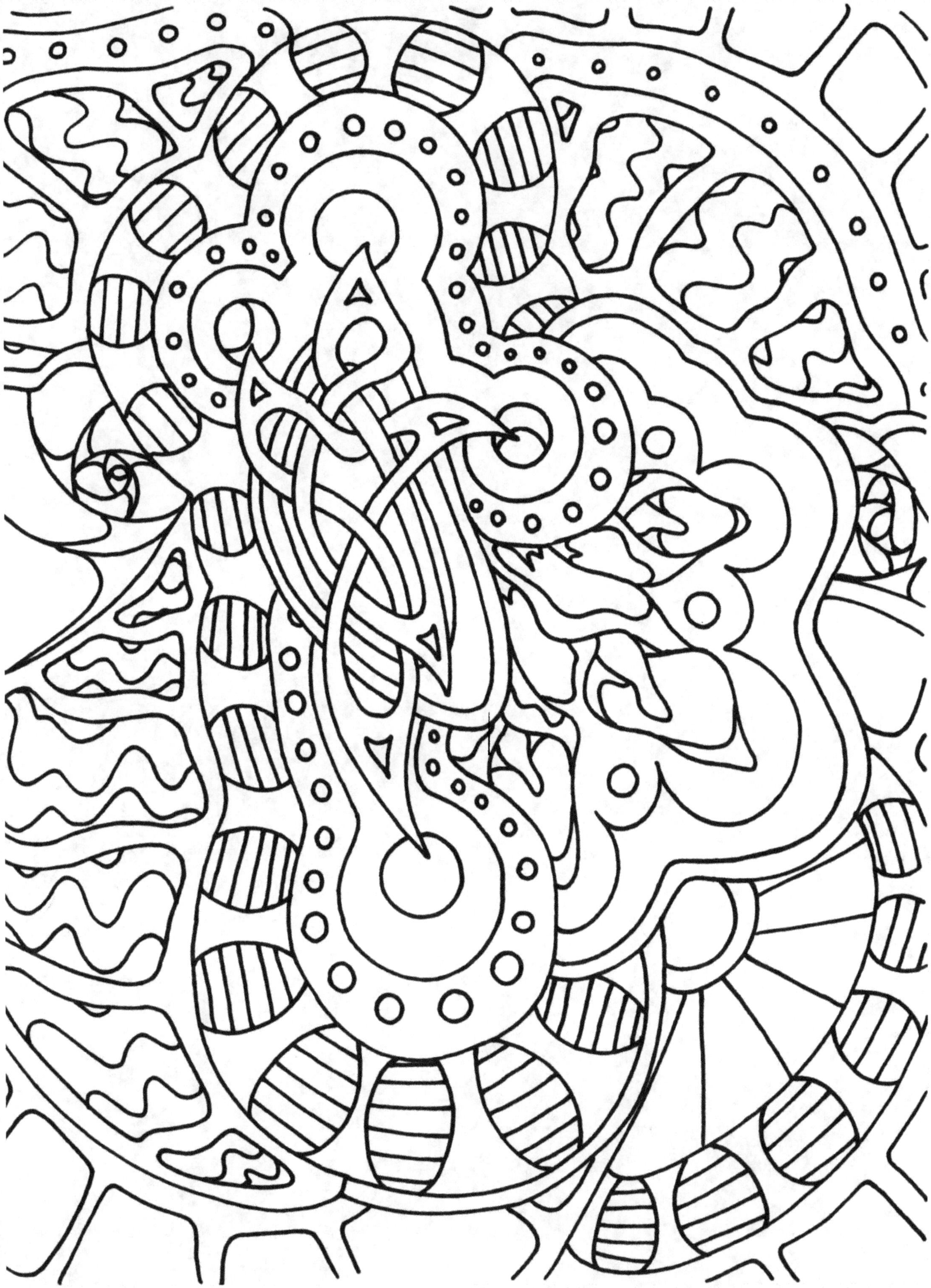

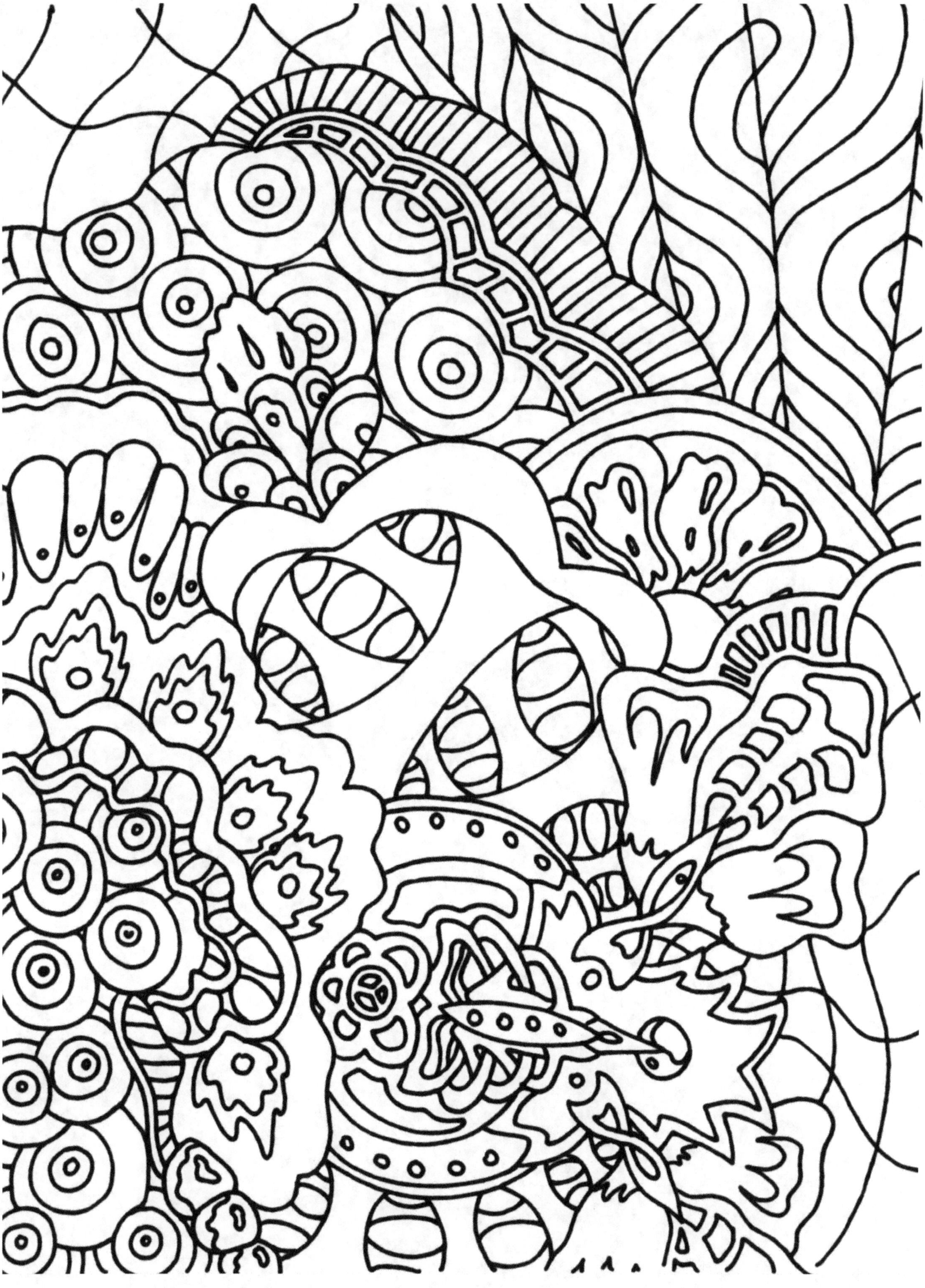

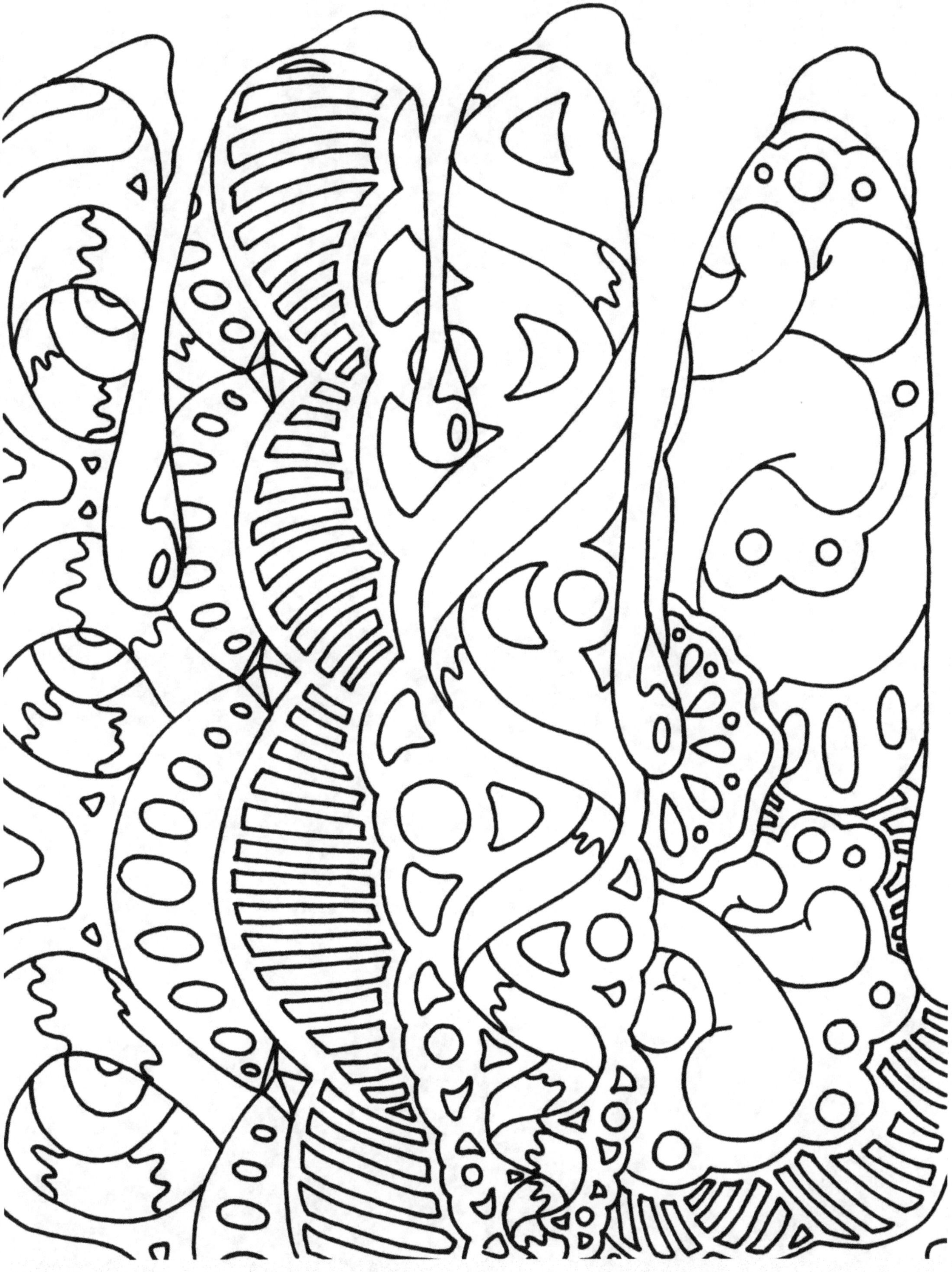

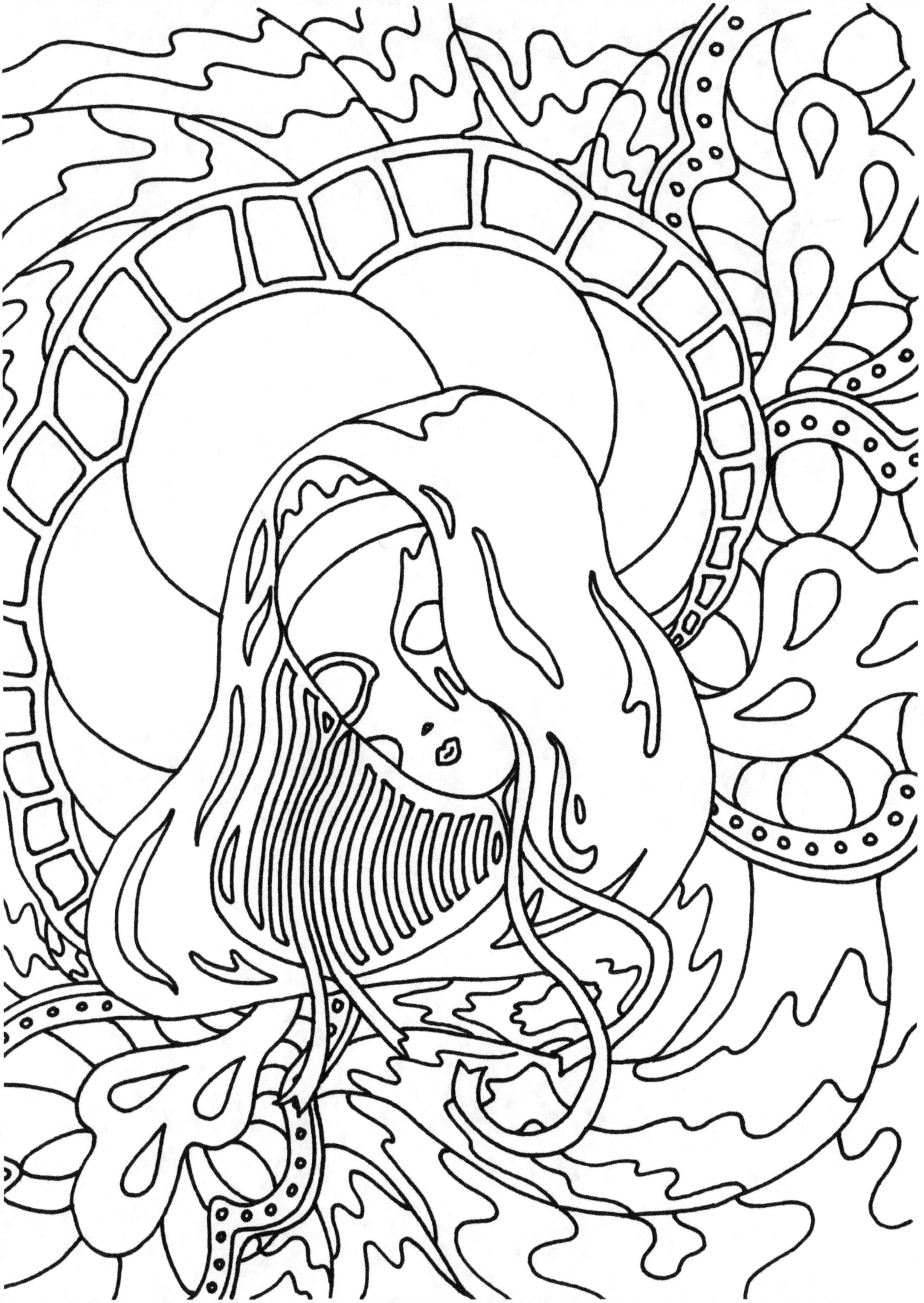

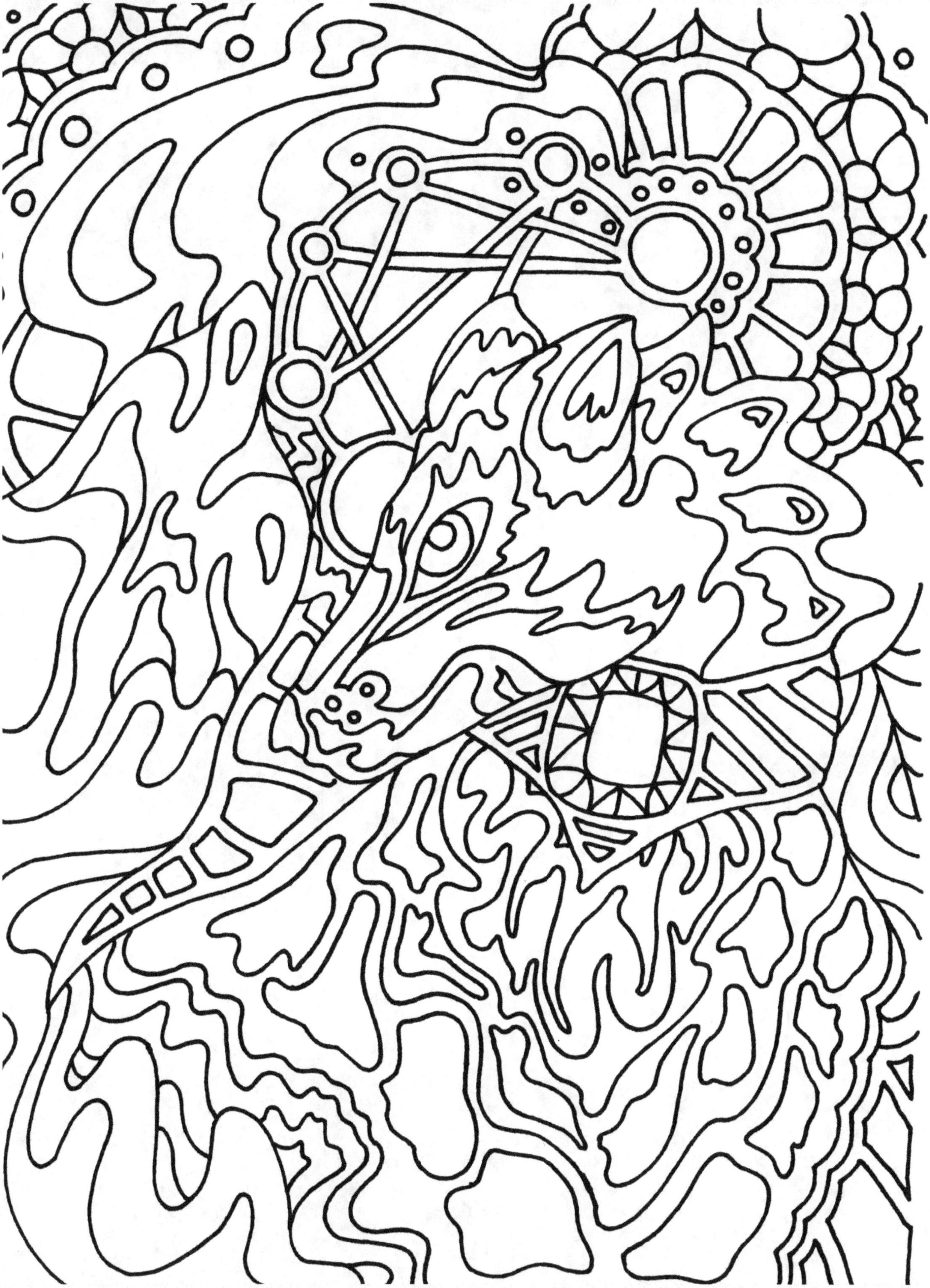

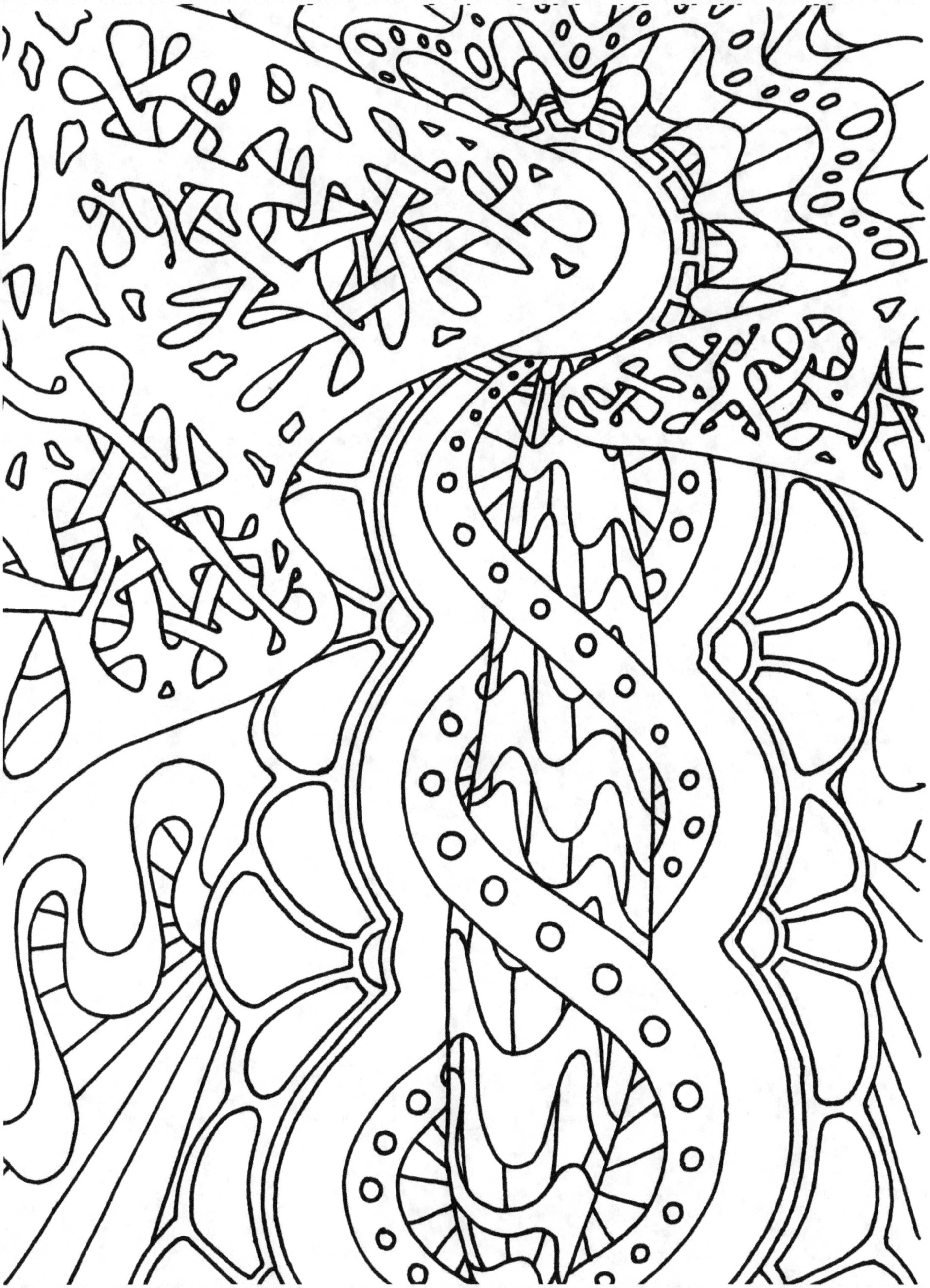

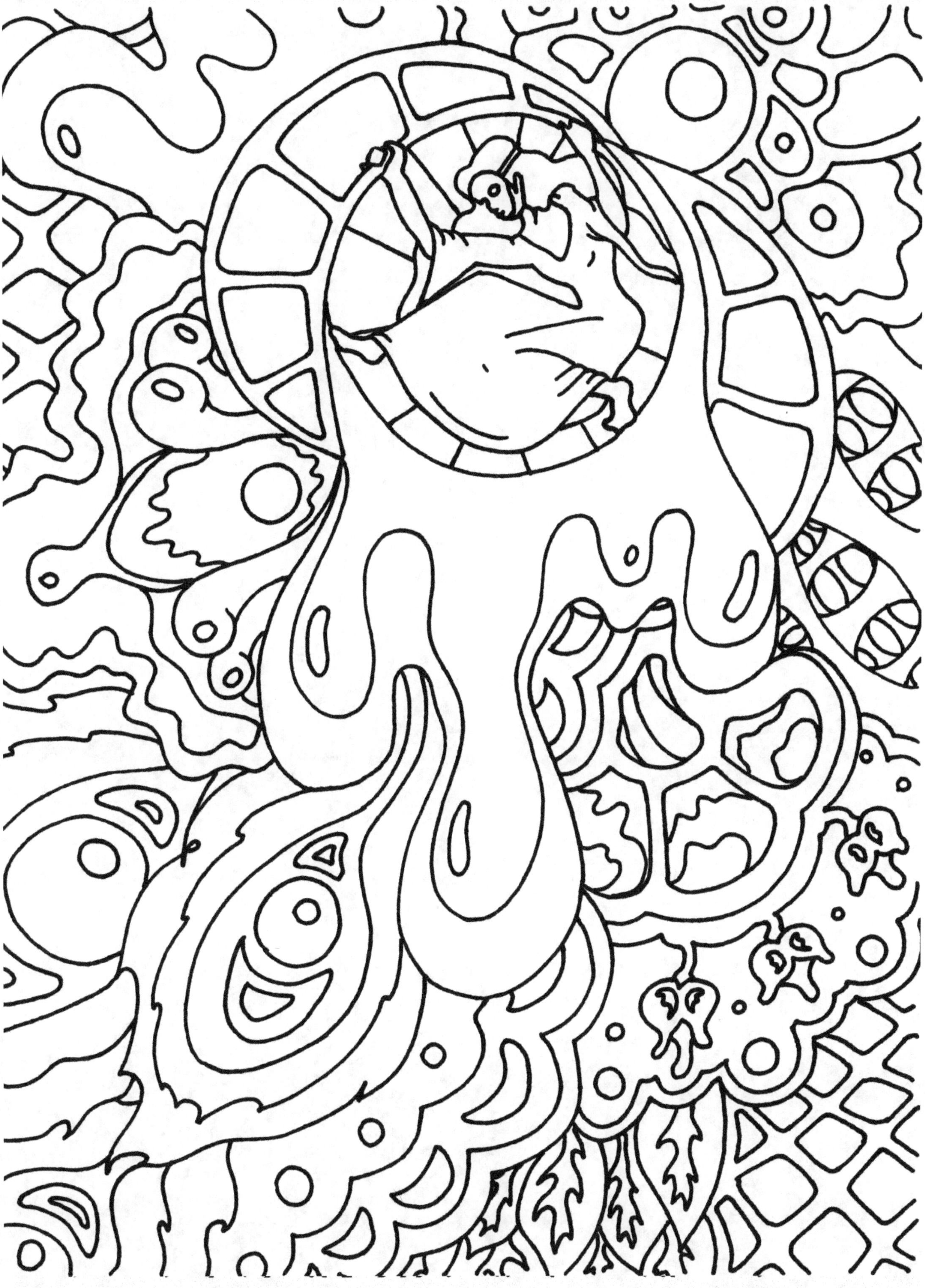

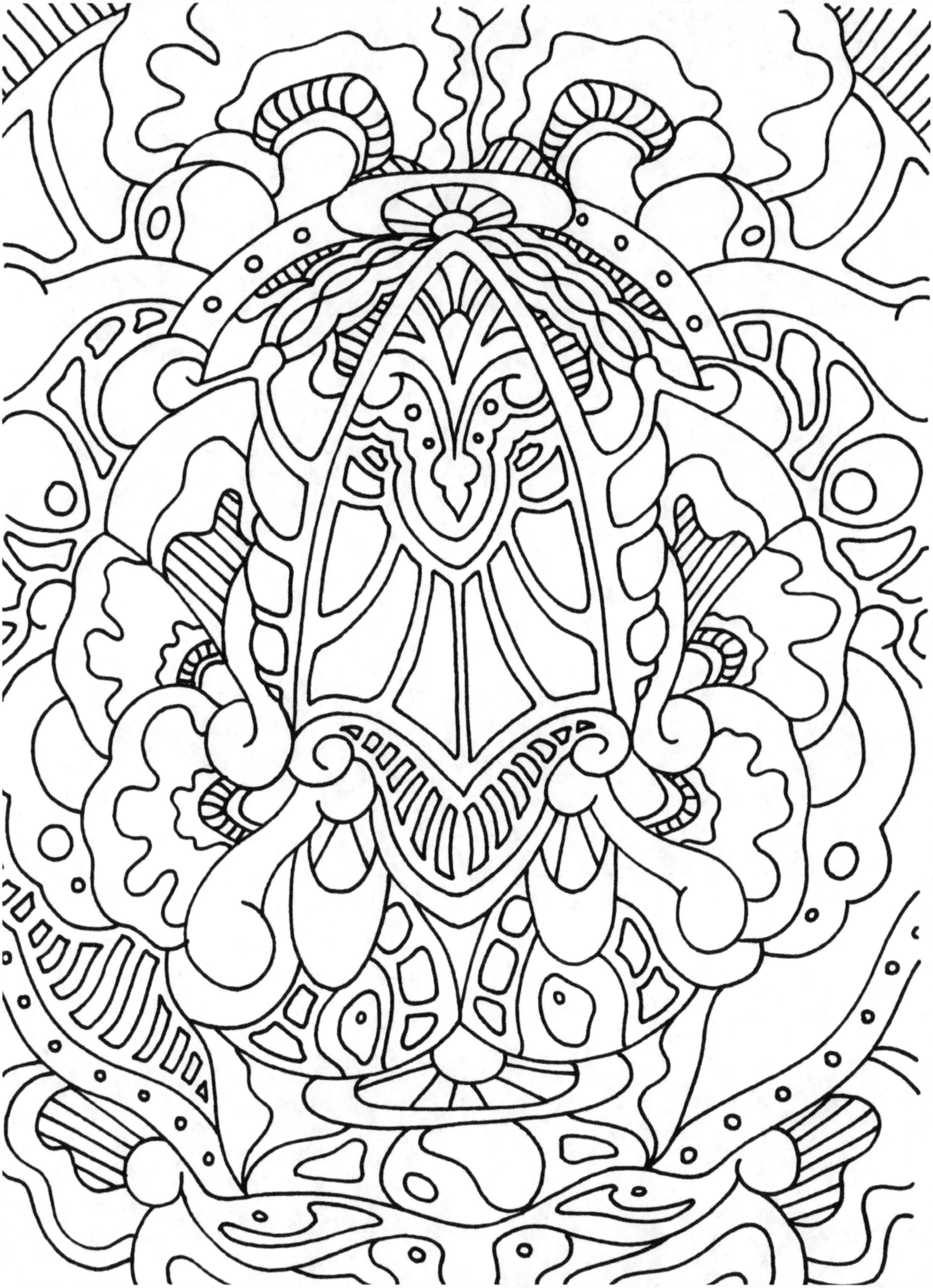

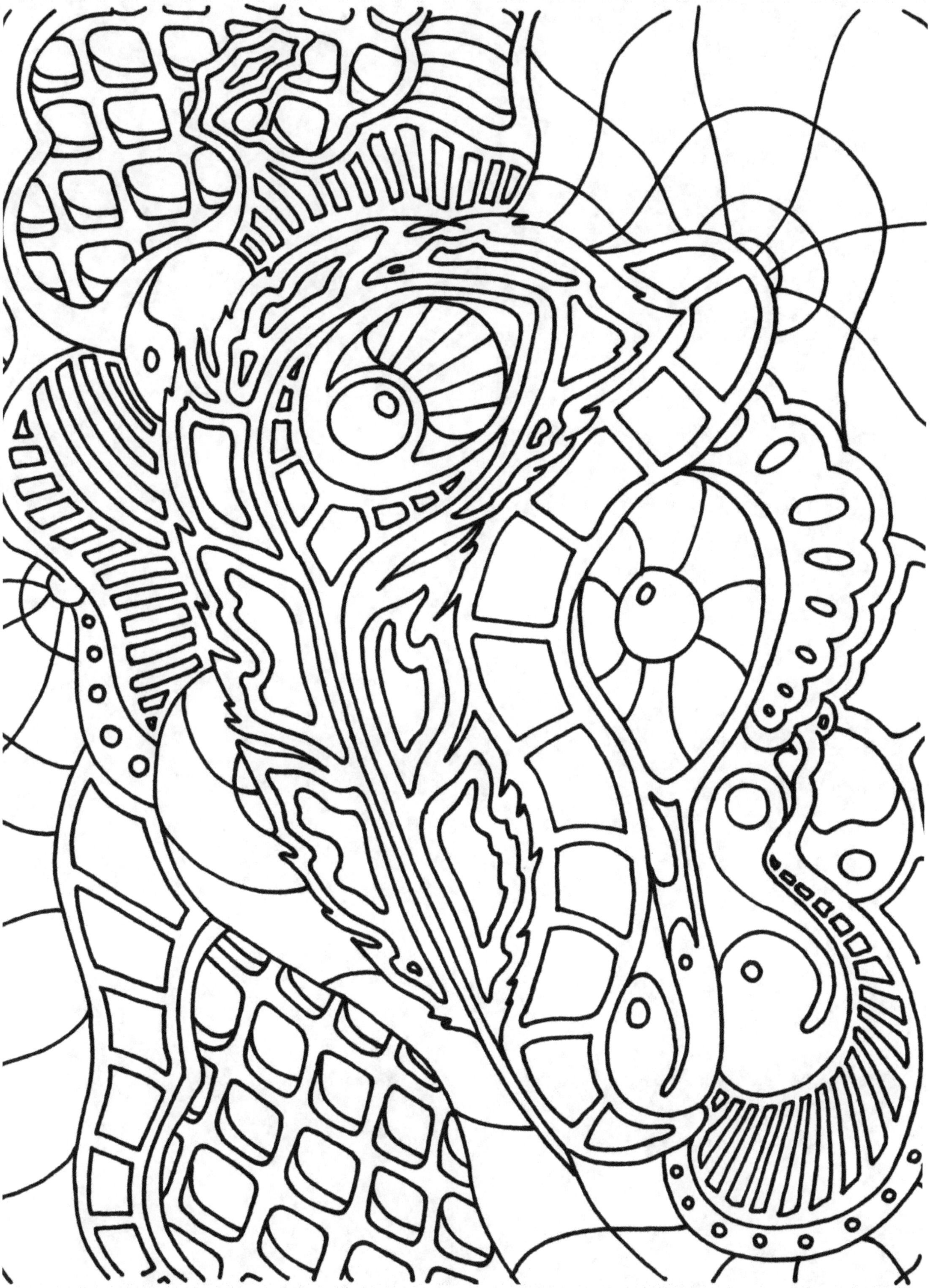

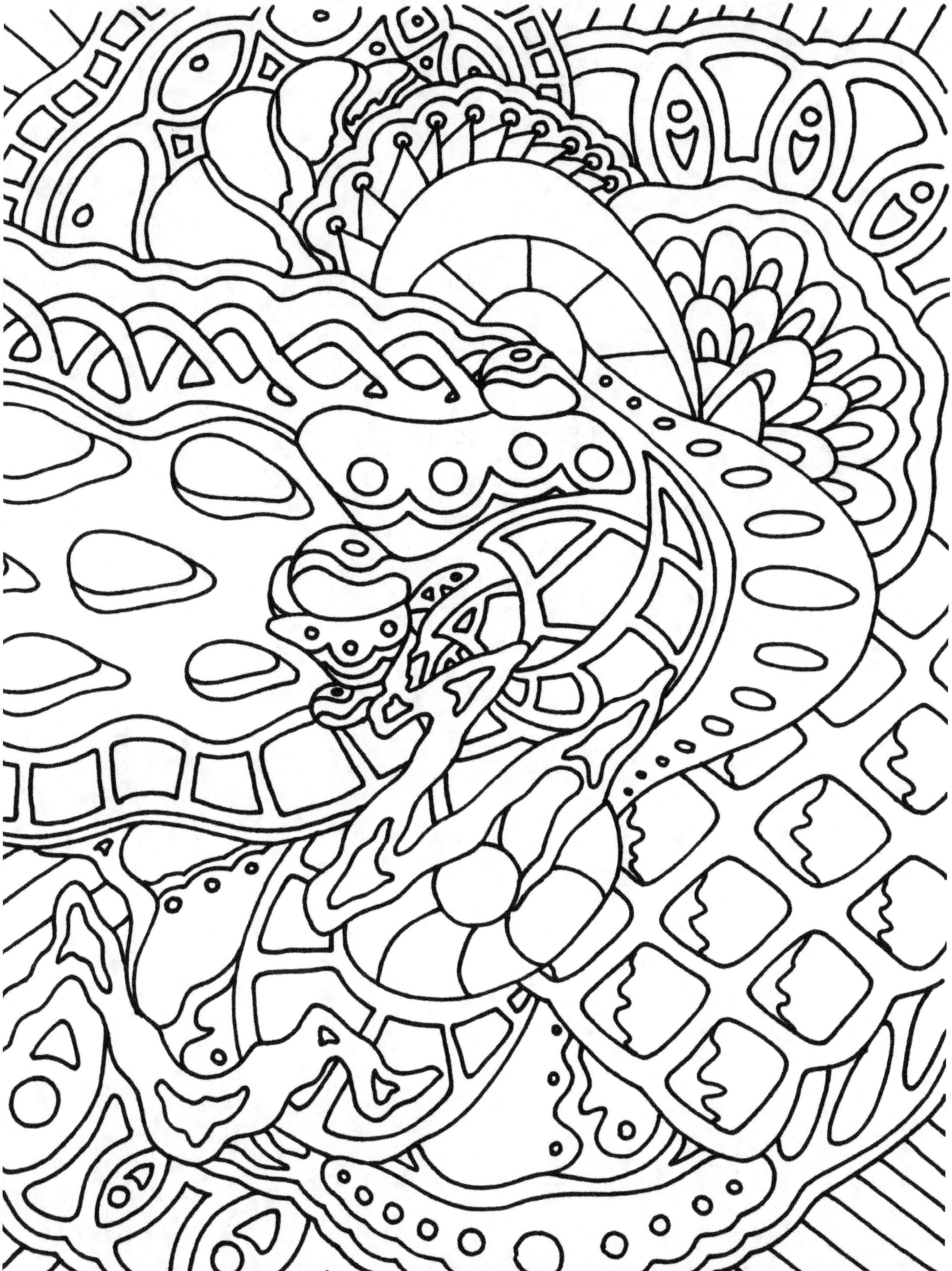

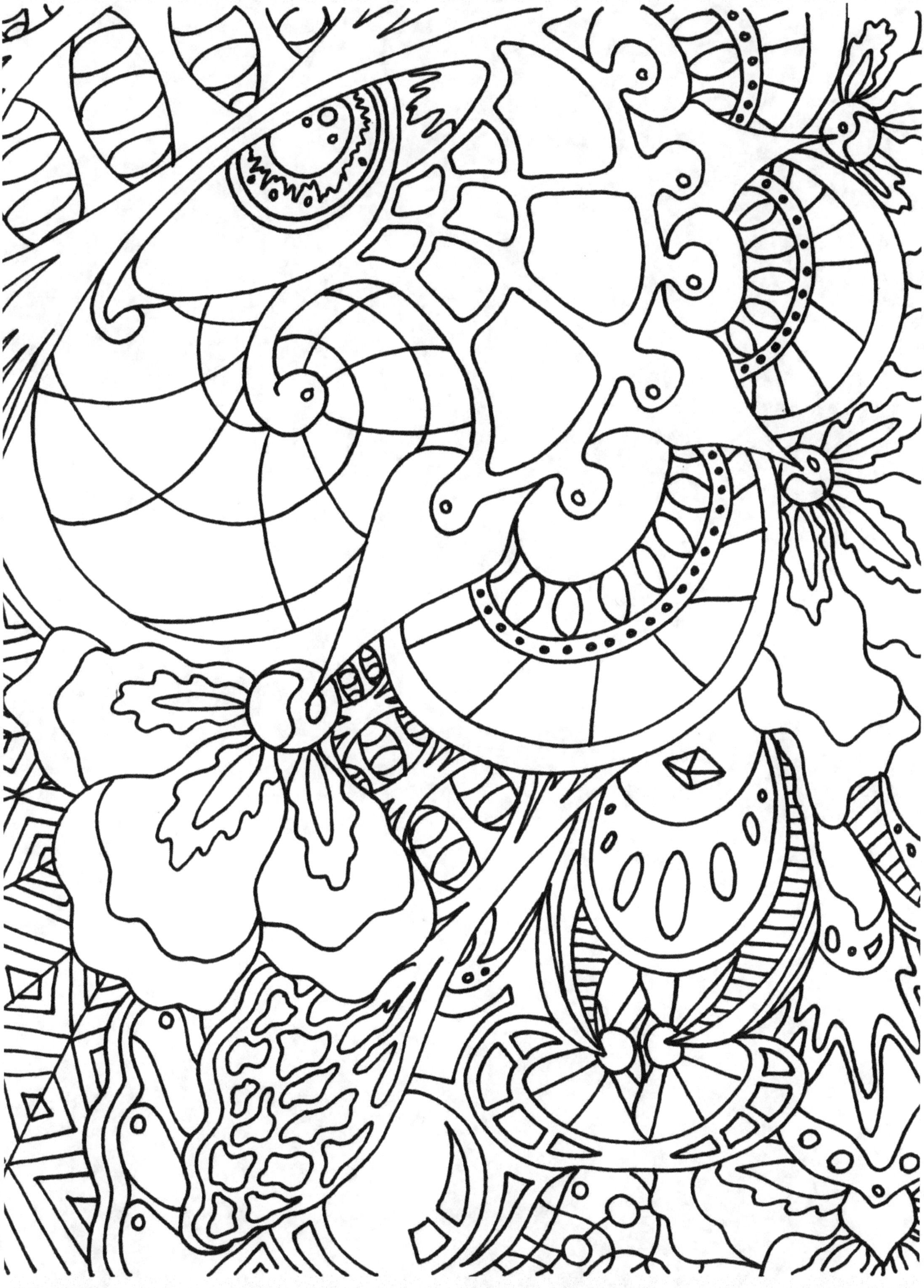

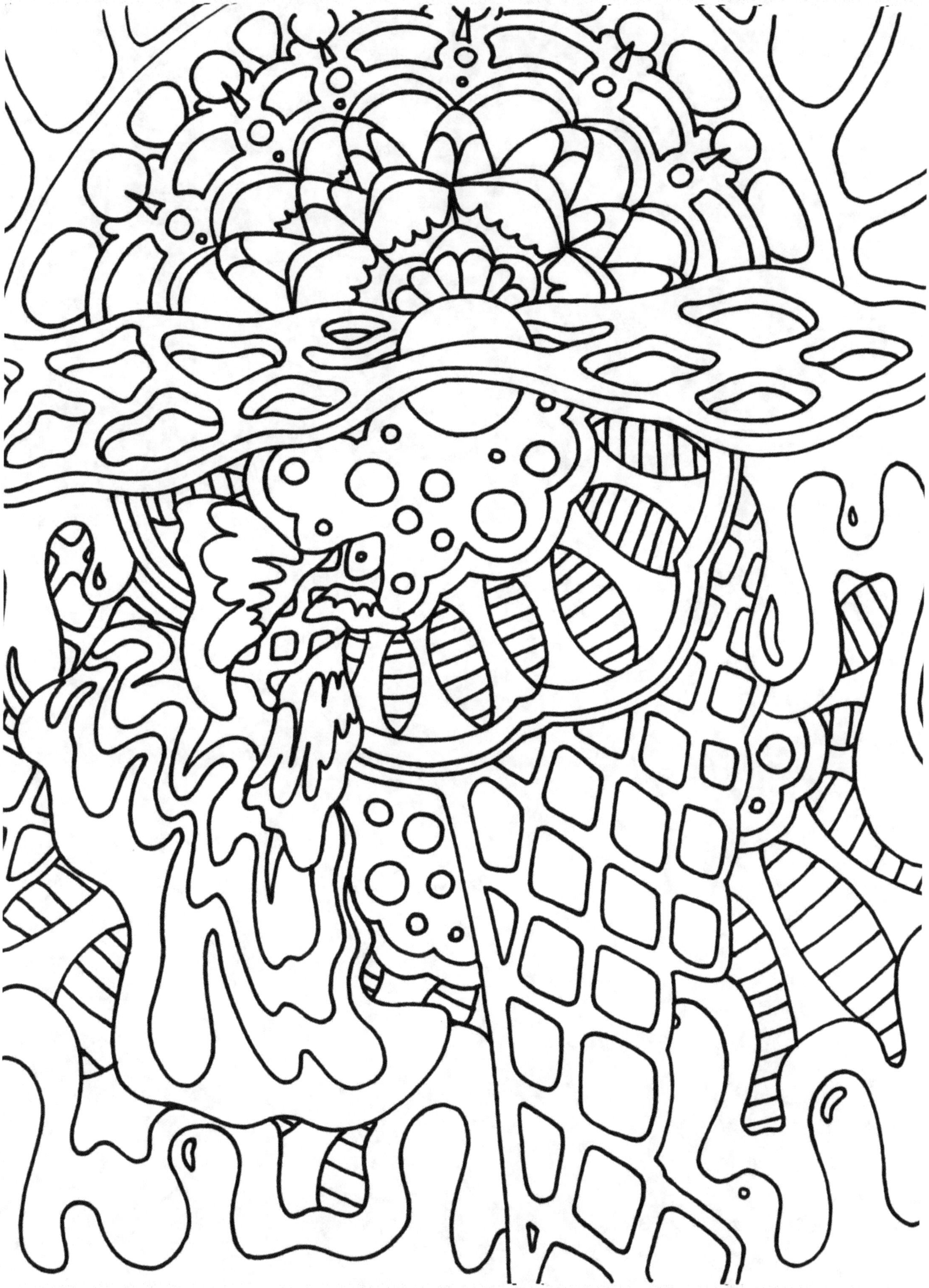

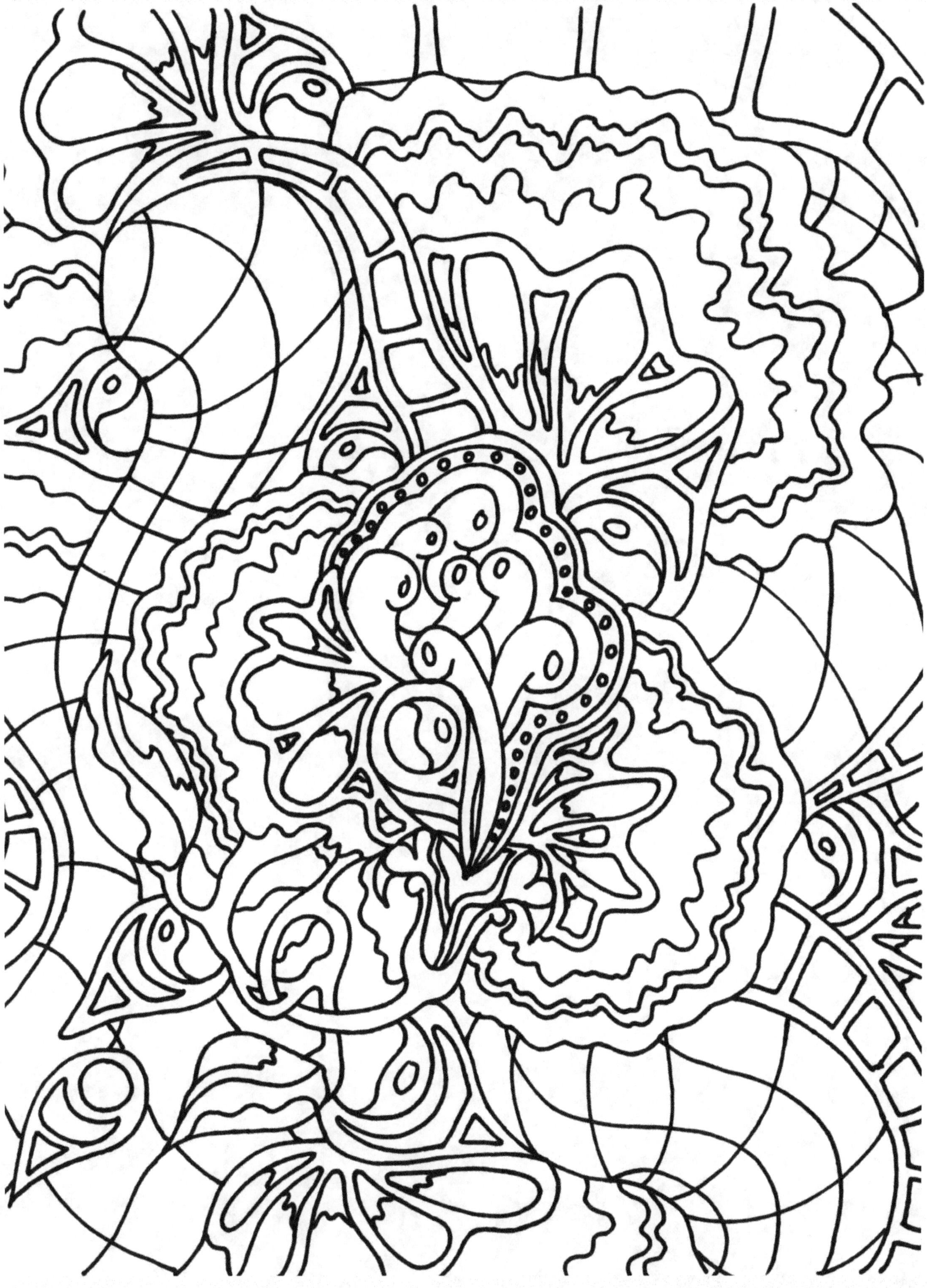

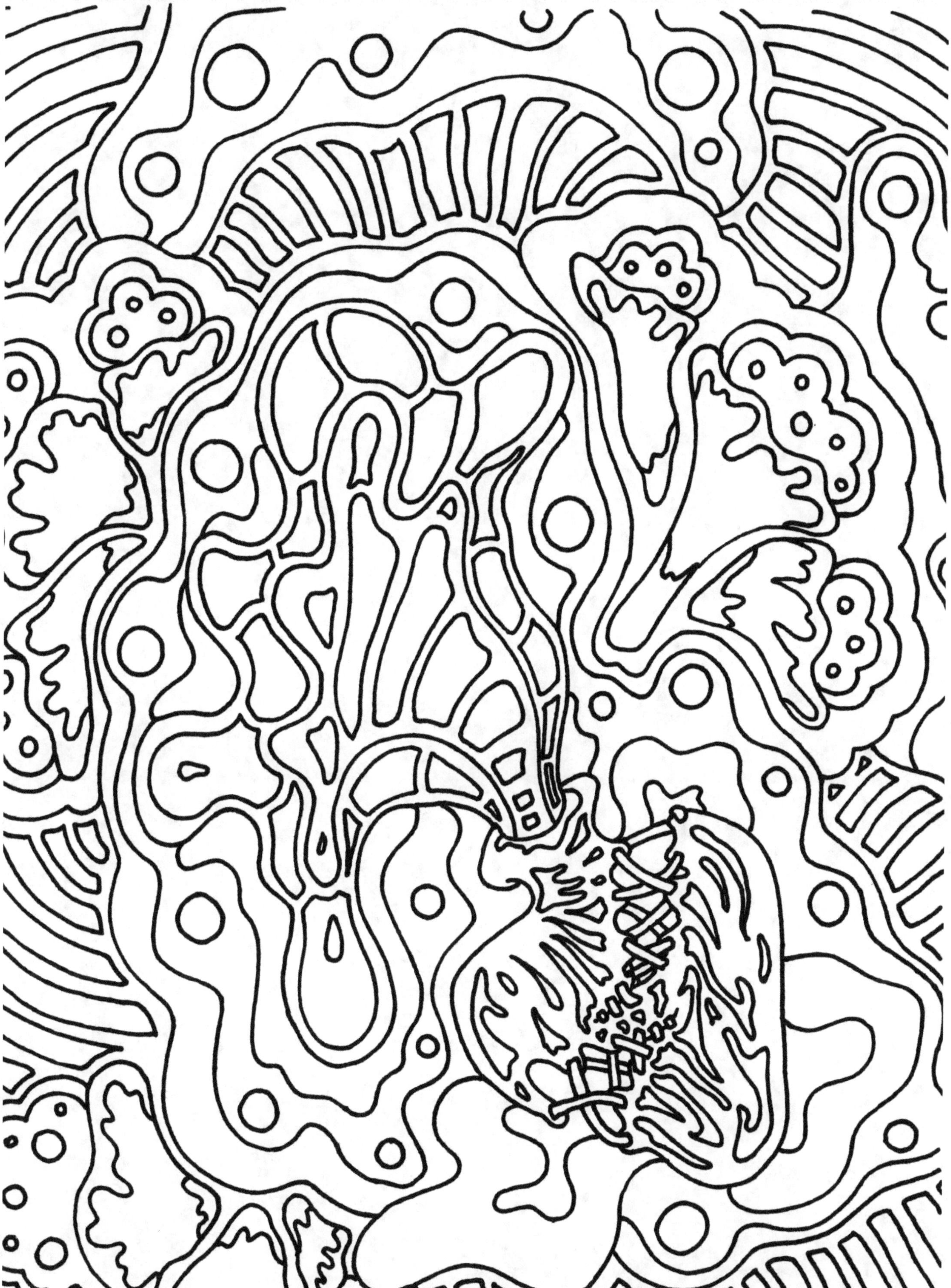

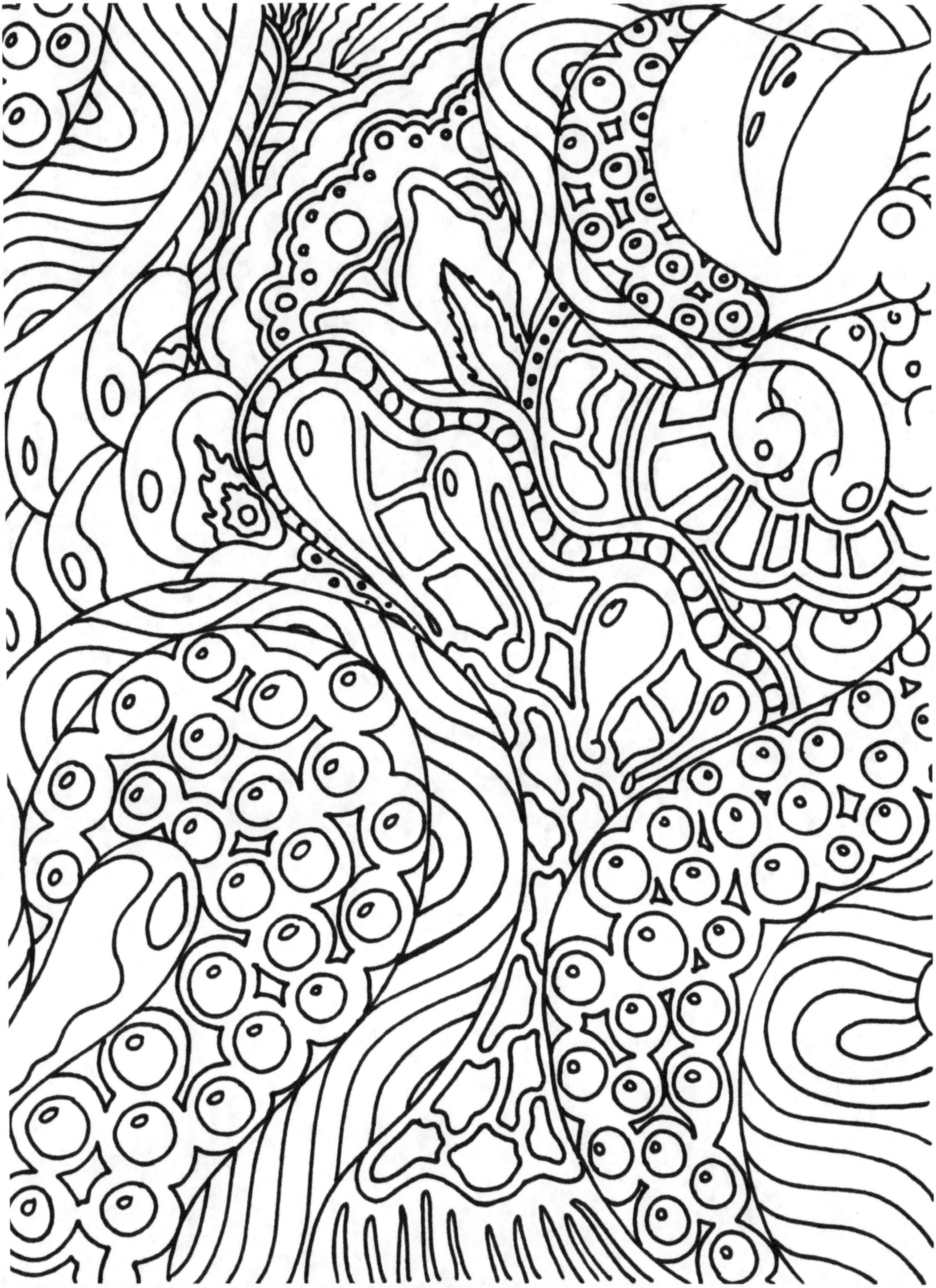

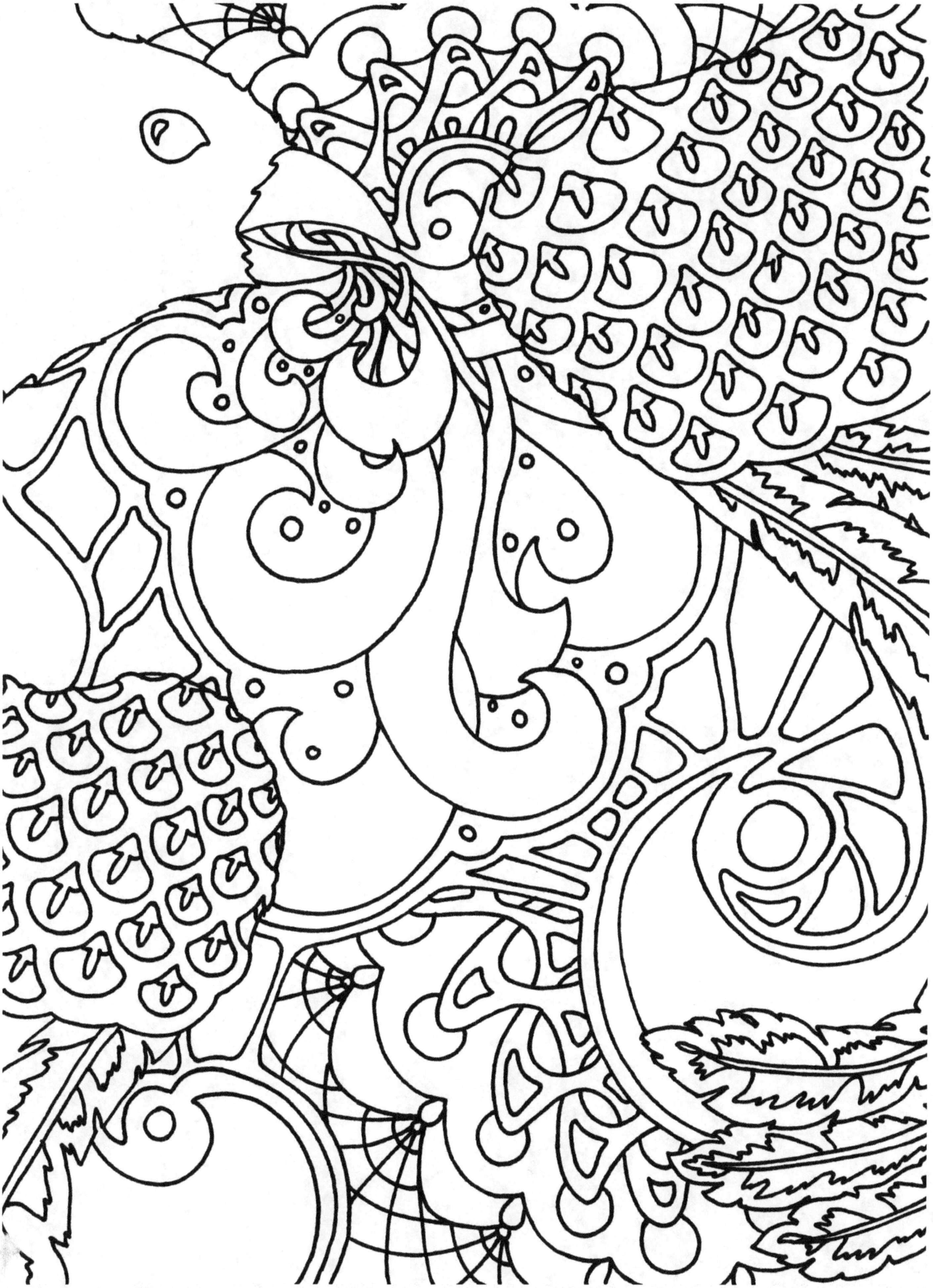

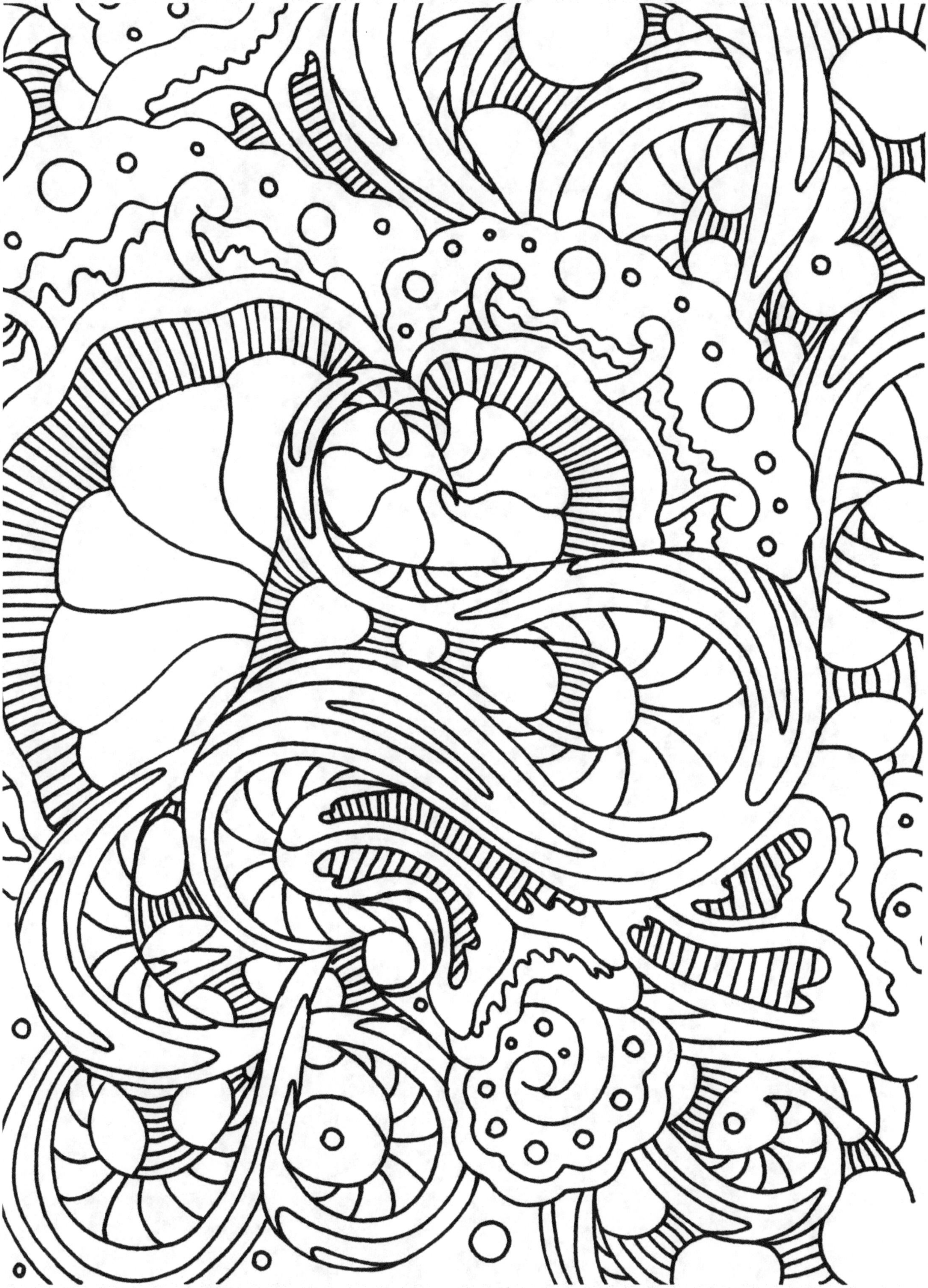

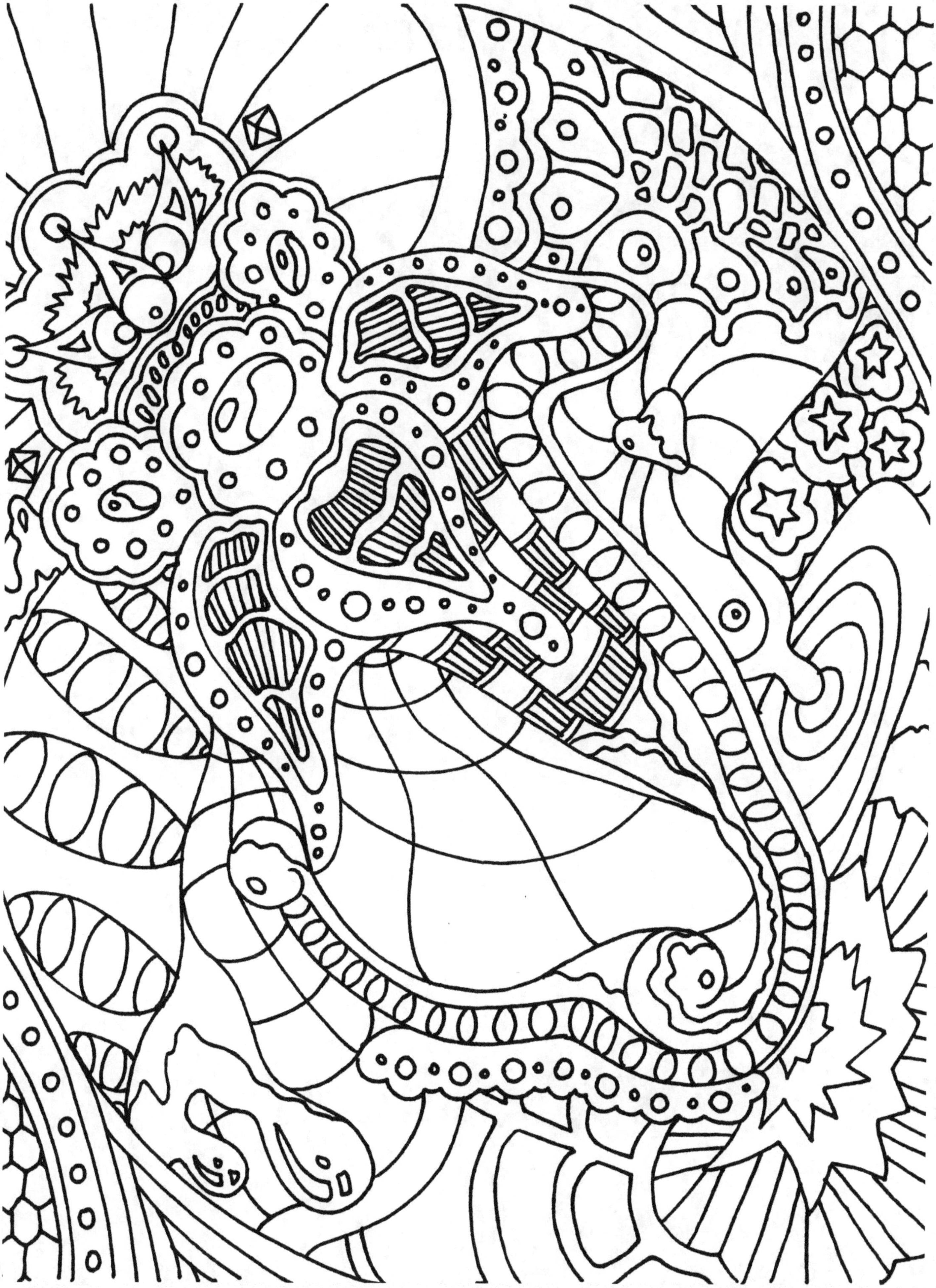

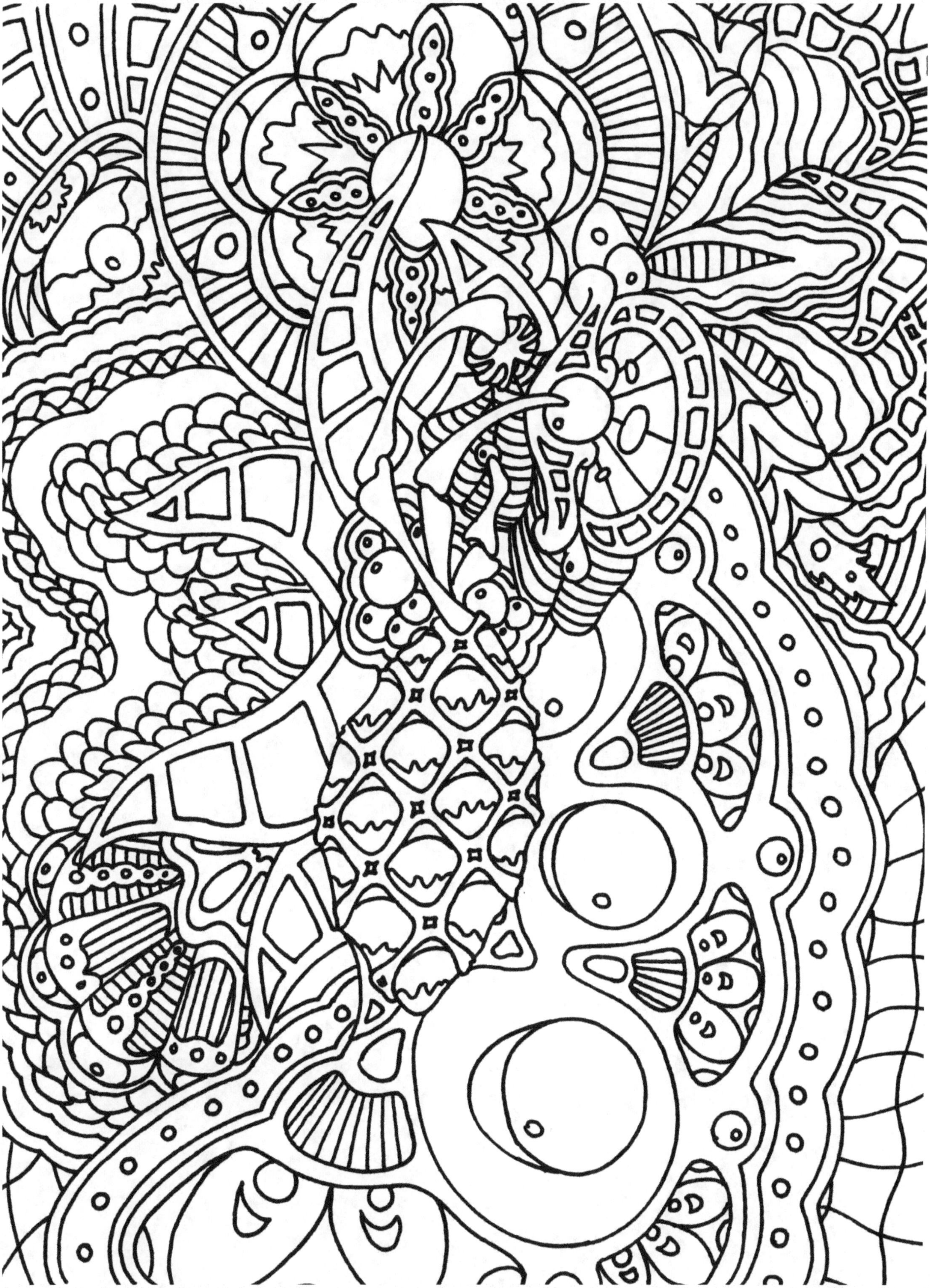

Swatch Page

Test your colors

www.ingramcontent.com/pod-product-compliance
Lightning Source LLC
Chambersburg PA
CBHW080946170526
45158CB00008B/2397
* 9 7 8 0 6 9 2 0 9 7 7 5 5 *